School Leader's Guide to Tackling Attendance Challenges is an invaluable resource for developing an effective and sustainable strategy for reducing chronic absence. Combining research summaries and inspiring success stories with concrete advice, examples, and tools, it is a clear and compelling read that will help any administrator determine how to ensure students show up to class every day—so that they can learn and succeed.

Hedy N. Chang
Executive Director, Attendance Works

SCHOOL LEADER'S
GUIDE TO
TACKLING
ATTENDANCE
CHALLENGES

SCHOOL LEADER'S
GUIDE TO
TACKLING
ATTENDANCE
CHALLENGES

JESSICA **SPRICK** | RANDY **SPRICK**

Arlington, VA USA

Eugene, Oregon USA

2800 Shirlington Rd., Suite 1001 • Arlington, VA 22206 USA
Phone: 800-933-2723 or 703-578-9600 • Fax: 703-575-5400
Website: www.ascd.org • E-mail: member@ascd.org
Author guidelines: www.ascd.org/write

21 West 6th Avenue
Eugene, Oregon 97401 USA
Phone: 866-542-1490 • Fax: 541-345-1507
Website: www.ancorapublishing.com

Deborah S. Delisle, *Executive Director;* Stefani Roth, *Publisher;* Genny Ostertag, *Director, Content Acquisitions;* Susan Hills, *Acquisitions Editor;* Julie Houtz, *Director, Book Editing & Production;* Darcie Russell, *Editor;* Judi Connelly, *Associate Art Director;* Masie Chong, *Graphic Designer;* Circle Graphics, *Typesetter;* Mike Kalyan, *Director, Production Services;* Trinay Blake, *E-Publishing Specialist.*

PAPERBACK ISBN: 978-1-4166-2681-7   ASCD product #118037 n10/18
PDF E-BOOK ISBN: 978-1-4166-2683-1; see Books in Print for other formats.
Quantity discounts are available: e-mail programteam@ascd.org or call 800-933-2723, ext. 5773, or 703-575-5773. For desk copies, go to www.ascd.org/deskcopy.

Library of Congress Cataloging-in-Publication Data

Names: Sprick, Jessica, author. | Sprick, Randall S., author.
Title: School leader's guide to tackling attendance challenges / Jessica
  Sprick, Randy Sprick.
Description: Alexandria, Virginia : ASCD, 2019. | Includes bibliographical
  references and index.
Identifiers: LCCN 2018025773 (print) | LCCN 2018027767 (ebook) | ISBN
  9781416626831 (PDF) | ISBN 9781416626817 (pbk.)
Subjects: LCSH: School attendance—United States. | School
  environment--United States. | School management and organization—United
  States.
Classification: LCC LB3081 (ebook) | LCC LB3081 .S67 2018 (print) | DDC
  371.2/94—dc23
LC record available at https://lccn.loc.gov/2018025773

28 27 26 25 24 23   5 6 7 8 9 10 11 12

SCHOOL LEADER'S *GUIDE TO*
TACKLING ATTENDANCE CHALLENGES

Acknowledgments

Our thanks and appreciation to both ASCD and Ancora Publishing for agreeing to copublish this resource. Specifically, Susan Hills, Darcie Russell, and the entire ASCD team have provided support, guidance, and a true model of professional collegiality. From Ancora Publishing, Matt Sprick, Sara Ferris, and Natalie Conaway have provided invaluable assistance in guiding the development of this resource. Lastly, we owe deep debt to the many educators who field-tested our ideas and shared practical and creative ideas to enrich this book. Jake Alabiso, school psychologist from Barnes Elementary School, and Jeffrey Johnson, principal of Challenger High School, provided inspiring models of what can happen when skilled leaders and dedicated staff work together to improve student attendance.

Introduction

For students to be successful in school, they have to actually *be* in school. Despite the obvious nature of this statement, far too many students miss too much school, and student absenteeism has been largely overlooked in school and district efforts to improve student outcomes. Fortunately, that situation is rapidly changing.

In the past decade, a movement has been building to research and address chronic absenteeism (defined in this book as missing 10 percent of school days for any reason—excused absence, unexcused absence, suspension). The strong correlations and negative effects associated with chronic absence (discussed in Chapter 1) have led to increased attention from schools, districts, and state and federal policymakers, and a host of new initiatives are being implemented to improve student attendance. This book provides a comprehensive framework as well as concrete and practical strategies to guide your team in addressing this critical issue.

Tackling schoolwide attendance requires a paradigm shift in how we conceptualize the problem and implement prevention and intervention efforts to deal with chronic absence. To understand this shift, let's first consider the traditional approach to addressing absenteeism.

The Traditional Approach

Many schools collect data on absenteeism and have policies and procedures they implement when students reach certain thresholds of absenteeism.

The Metric of Truancy

In past models, schools identified absenteeism problems primarily by measures of truancy. However, truancy relates only to absences that occur *without* parent permission. Although measures of truancy are important because they are strongly associated with risk factors of disengagement and dropping out, they can be misleading. Many students have inordinate numbers of excused absences. Others may have a relatively low rate of absenteeism for each type of reason (excused, unexcused, and suspension), but when all absences are combined, these students exhibit patterns of problematic attendance. The extent of a school's absenteeism problem may not be apparent when looking solely at truancy metrics, especially in elementary schools.

Increasingly Punitive "Interventions"

In a traditional model, when a student is identified as having an absenteeism problem, the following may occur:

- At a certain number of unexcused absences (e.g., three), a letter is sent home to warn the student and parent that unexcused absences can lead to truancy court proceedings.
- At a certain number of additional unexcused absences (e.g., a total of five), the school initiates a parent meeting by phone or conducts an in-person conference to further warn about the punitive consequences of additional unexcused absences.
- At a state-mandated level (e.g., 10 unexcused absences or 5 in a one-month period), the school refers the student and student's family to juvenile court, and proceedings for a truancy hearing are initiated.
- If the court finds the student truant, the court orders penalties such as the following:
  - Fines or other penalties to the parent or guardian (e.g., a requirement to attend parent education courses or family counseling)
  - Detention or probation from school
  - Counseling
  - Drug testing
  - Dropout prevention or other courses

This primarily reactive and punitive approach was used by schools for decades despite limited positive effects. However, these methods provide intervention that is too little and too late for many students. Truancy courts may be an effective last step for a small number of students (we heard one story about a student whose school tried a host of positive and function-based interventions, but the only thing that changed his behavior was the threat of his parents receiving a large fine). For most students, however, we argue that truancy court is like heart bypass surgery. It is a last-stage effort used only in extreme cases where many other less costly, less complicated, and less risky preventive measures have already been tried.

Furthermore, we have heard from truancy court officers that their ability to provide meaningful intervention and follow-up is almost nonexistent because of the massive numbers of students who pass through the court system. The courts have to shuffle students through as quickly as possible because truancy court is often the main or only tool used by schools to address excessive absenteeism. If truancy court is to be an effective late-stage corrective action, we need to begin to shift our model from a reliance on reactive and punitive approaches to approaches that are multitiered and positive in focus, and that use proven principles of behavioral change.

Toward a New Model

Within the field of education, a vast body of research provides information about best practices for changing student behavior. Evidence-based approaches such as positive behavioral interventions and supports (PBIS) and functional behavioral assessment (FBA) may be more effective in changing student behavior than traditional reactive and punitive models like the truancy court example just described. The model of absenteeism prevention and intervention developed by our company, Safe & Civil Schools, takes what we already know about changing any problematic behavior (e.g., disruptive or defiant behavior) and applies it to address absenteeism. Some of the key components of this model include the following:

- A belief that behavior can be changed

- An increased focus on prevention and proactive measures

- An understanding that our efforts should attempt as much as possible to address causes of the problematic behavior

This book incorporates the following additional guiding principles:

- Schools should work to address all types of absenteeism, including excused, unexcused, and suspension-based absences.

- All stakeholders have a role to play in efforts to address absenteeism, including all staff members (administrators, teachers, paraprofessionals, and other classified and certified staff), students, families, and even community members.
- We cannot punish students into wanting to attend school!

The Safe & Civil Schools approach applies a Multitiered System of Support (MTSS) model to address attendance and truancy problems in school. This model focuses on creating a continuum of support that ensures that no student falls through the cracks. In an MTSS approach, a team tailors the intensity of services provided to the intensity of student need; no student receives more individualized services than he or she needs, and no student with a need for support goes unidentified or underserved.

The MTSS triangle (Figure 1) represents three tiers of support that should be in place, and the shape of the triangle depicts the goal for the proportion of students who fall into each of the three tiers when your prevention and intervention systems are functioning effectively. The foundation of the triangle—Tier 1—is the universal schoolwide and classroom

FIGURE 1 **Multitiered System of Support (MTSS) Triangle**

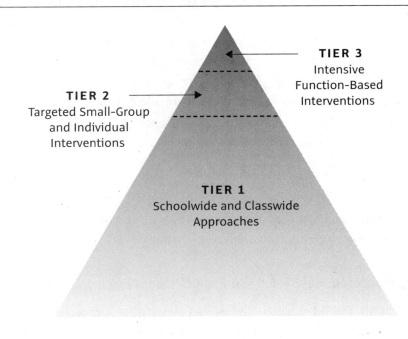

TIER 3
Intensive
Function-Based
Interventions

TIER 2
Targeted Small-Group
and Individual
Interventions

TIER 1
Schoolwide and Classwide
Approaches

systems that prevent absenteeism problems within the vast majority of your student body—80 to 90 percent. If many students in your school have problematic attendance behaviors, and intervening individually would overwhelm your intervention systems, increase your focus on universal prevention strategies. Chapters 2 through 9 focus on universal procedures such as developing an attendance team and monitoring data; engaging and supporting staff; and teaching students, families, and community about the importance of school attendance. Universal prevention also includes tailored strategies to address schoolwide priorities (Chapter 8) so that you can identify common causes of absenteeism in your school and apply appropriate schoolwide or classroom strategies to address those causes. The final universal chapter (Chapter 9) provides recommendations for how to analyze your attendance policies and refine them across time to address absenteeism issues in your school.

Chapters 10 and 11 provide Tier 2 and Tier 3 strategies for intervening with students whose absenteeism has been resistant to the universal Tier 1 approaches in your school. Because the focus of this book is on schoolwide processes and procedures, these chapters provide a brief overview of fairly complex procedures, offering a general sense of next steps for your team as they develop supports for students with resistant absenteeism issues. In some cases, you may find that simple modifications to existing intervention procedures for behavioral and academic issues at Tier 2 and Tier 3 may be appropriate for students with absenteeism problems.

How to Use This Book

School Leader's Guide to Tackling Attendance Challenges is designed as a resource guide to walk your school- or district-based team through all aspects of implementing a systematic, multitiered approach to absenteeism prevention and intervention. Designed for use with school-based teams such as PBIS teams, leadership teams, and attendance teams or task forces, this book can also be used by district and building administrators, school board members, and other policymakers who seek to improve attendance, address academic achievement, or increase funding that is tied to attendance. Throughout the book you will find practical strategies and tools for implementing the general research-based recommendations. The book also includes many real-world examples of successful approaches used by schools to address absenteeism through multitiered systems.

A forthcoming companion resource for teachers, *Teacher's Guide to Tackling Attendance Challenges*, will provide significantly expanded classroom resources such as sample lesson plans for a variety of common attendance issues, ready-to-go reinforcement systems, and talking points for teachers to use with students and families. Although the *School Leader's Guide* can be used on its own to design your overarching system, you may decide to provide teachers with copies of the *Teacher's Guide* to reduce the workload of the school team.

K–12 Applications

The overarching procedures described in this book are applicable from kindergarten through grade 12. Although we have provided examples across all grade levels, we emphasize early intervention in primary and elementary grades as well as the middle school transition. When absenteeism problems in elementary school or early middle school are not addressed, additional related problems can occur in later middle school and high school, when prevention and intervention become more complex. For example, what may be a simple problem in elementary school, such as lack of understanding about the importance of attendance or lack of reliable transportation, may result in the student falling behind academically and disengaging from adults or peers if left unaddressed. The longer the problem goes on, the more complex, difficult, and resource intensive the intervention becomes. This book emphasizes the importance of starting the work of building a schoolwide culture of attendance as early as preK and kindergarten.

Addressing Tardies

The approaches described in this book can be easily modified to address excessive morning tardies (e.g., when large numbers of students arrive 30 minutes to an hour late in the morning) or excessive end-of-day absences (e.g., when large numbers of students are picked up from school before the end of the school day). If these kinds of tardies or time-of-day absences are problematic for students in your school, consider how you can modify strategies such as educating students and families, motivational systems, and other universal schoolwide and classroom systems described in Chapters 2 through 9 to address the problem. If individual students struggle with tardiness, see the strategies in Chapters 10 and 11 for Tier 2 and Tier 3 approaches.

■ ■ ■ ■ ■

For far too long, attendance was viewed as something that was beyond a school's control: "It's a parent problem" or "She's just unmotivated, so there's really nothing we can do to make her come to school." However, emerging research and the experiences that we've had working with schools to implement positive, proactive, and multitiered approaches to absenteeism issues have shown us that this issue is far from beyond schools' control. In fact, schools have great power to effect positive change. When all members of the school community work together to create a culture of attendance, the results can be immense. Let's get started!

1

Understanding the Stakes: Why We Should Address Chronic Absence

Many teachers and other school staff suffer from *initiative fatigue*. As schools and districts work to address a multitude of academic and other priorities, it can be difficult to get the buy-in required for any initiative to succeed. This is especially true if turnover in leadership produces rapid changes in focus, causing some people to feel that initiatives are fleeting and have limited potential to create meaningful change. Although many people may acknowledge the difficulties created by frequent student absences, your team may experience resistance from staff members who feel that even this initiative is just "one more thing" that won't yield long-lasting improvements for them or their students. In this chapter we present research and other rationales to help answer the crucial question, "Why should we address chronic absence?" This information can help staff members understand that tackling attendance will positively affect academic and behavioral outcomes. The goal is to get your team to believe that this initiative is something that will significantly improve student outcomes, classrooms, and personal job satisfaction.

To begin, we summarize current findings on the prevalence and variability of rates of chronic absence. We also provide information on the negative effects of absenteeism that are supported by research and that we have heard repeatedly from educators across the United States. These effects occur for the student, the class and school, and the families, community, and society at large.

Read this chapter for a broad overview and confirmation of why it is important to invest in efforts to address absenteeism. This chapter has a heavy emphasis on citing the existing research base on chronic absenteeism for those of you who will be tasked to "make a case" to your district that this is a critical initiative for your school or district to tackle. Subsequent chapters focus less on theory and research and more on practical implementation strategies. You may want to return to this chapter when you work through Chapter 4, "Engaging and Supporting Staff in Attendance Efforts," as you determine what information to share with staff. You may also decide to select and share relevant information from this chapter with students, families, and your community.

The Prevalence of Chronic Absence in U.S. Schools

Until recently, it was unclear how widespread chronic absence was in schools across the United States. Based on data from six states that calculated and reported rates of chronic absence, Balfanz and Byrnes (2012) estimated that 10 to 15 percent of students, or roughly 5 to 7.5 million students, were chronically absent. The 2013–2014 data set from the U.S. Department of Education Office for Civil Rights (2016) was the first to report nationwide absence rates. These data indicated that approximately 14 percent of the student population—more than 6.5 million students—missed 15 days or more of school. Although this threshold is slightly lower than the 18 days of absence across a school year that is typically used to identify chronic absentees, it clearly indicates that far too many students are missing critical amounts of school. The following section provides key findings about the variability of absenteeism across different populations and schools.

Variations Across States and Within States and Districts

The data show that absenteeism varies significantly across states and within states and districts. Although absenteeism is widespread across the United States, certain geographic locations clearly have increased rates. The Office for Civil Rights found that 500 districts reported that 30 percent or more of their student body missed 15 days of school or more. Attendance Works and the Everyone Graduates Center (2017) noted that these districts were not evenly spread across the nation. State data ranged from 2 to 29 percent of schools having 30 percent or more of their student body absent 15 days or more. Furthermore, although nationwide data indicated that chronic absenteeism may be more likely in urban areas, individual states were more variable. For example, rates of chronic absence in California and Wyoming were higher in rural districts. Although researchers did not definitively attribute a cause to this variability, one key variable strongly correlated with absenteeism is rate of poverty. Districts and states with higher rates of poverty, regardless of whether they are urban, suburban, or rural, are likely to experience higher rates of chronic absence.

The Correlation Between Poverty and Absenteeism

Students who live in poverty are more likely to exhibit patterns of chronic absence (Attendance Works and the Everyone Graduates Center, 2017; Balfanz & Byrnes, 2012; Ginsberg, Chang, & Jordan, 2014). For example, in Nebraska, two-thirds of chronically absent students were found to be economically disadvantaged (Balfanz & Byrnes, 2012). In Utah, students from low-income homes (who received free or reduced lunch) were 90 percent more likely to be chronically absent than students who were not from low-income homes (Utah Education Policy Center, 2012). Balfanz and Byrnes (2012) conclude that one of the most effective ways to help get students out of situations of poverty is to get them to attend school each day.

Additional Trends

Note: Unless otherwise specified, the following findings are taken from the Office for Civil Rights Data Collection for 2013–2014.

The following are a few additional trends to be aware of.

Absenteeism increases throughout middle and high school. Eleven percent of elementary students, 12.5 percent of middle school students, and 18.9 percent of high school students are chronically absent. These findings are similar to those from Balfanz and Byrnes (2012), who found that chronic absence gets steadily worse throughout middle school and high school. Balfanz and Byrnes also found that chronic absenteeism was high in kindergarten and 1st grade (approximately 10 percent), then became steadily better in grades 2 through 5, with a low of 5 percent of students in grade 5, according to data from multiple states and the Early Childhood Longitudinal Study of Kindergarten (ECLS-K).

Chronic absenteeism is more prevalent for specific minority groups. Across grades, 7.1 percent of Asian students, 12.7 percent white students, and 14.7 percent of Latino students missed 15 days or more in comparison with 22.5 percent of American Indian or Alaska Native students, 21.4 percent of Native Hawaiian or other Pacific Islander students, 17.3 percent of black students, and 16.4 percent of multiracial students. By high school, 20 percent or more of students who were not Asian or white were chronically absent: American Indian or Alaska Native—27 percent; Native Hawaiian or other Pacific Islander—25 percent; black—23 percent; multiracial—21 percent; and Latino—21 percent.

Chronic absenteeism is more prevalent for students with disabilities. Nineteen percent of students with disabilities were chronically absent, in comparison with 12.9 percent of students without disabilities.

There are no significant differences in chronic absence rates by gender. Approximately 14 percent of both male and female students were chronically absent.

Students who are highly mobile (foster children, children whose parents have migratory work, students who are homeless) are more likely to have problematic attendance. The Utah Education Policy Center (2012) found that mobile students (those who were unenrolled from one school and then reenrolled in another during a school year) were four times more likely, and homeless students were 2.5 times more likely, to be chronically absent than students who were not mobile or homeless.

How Irregular Attendance Negatively Affects Absent Students

Irregular attendance can have several damaging effects on students with frequent absences, including an increased likelihood of negative academic outcomes, possible exacerbation of problems with behavior and social-emotional aspects of school, and increased risk of negative behaviors and activities outside school. The next sections examine each of these possible effects.

Negative Academic Outcomes

Poorer student performance due to absenteeism begins as early as kindergarten and extends across grades, creating a cumulative effect. In analyses of data from the kindergarten cohort of the Early

Childhood Longitudinal Study, Romero and Lee (2007) found that students with greater absenteeism in kindergarten had the lowest academic performance in 1st grade. Students who missed 10 percent or more of the school year scored approximately 5 percentage points lower on reading performance, math performance, and measures of general knowledge than peers with low rates of absenteeism.

A study in California of three large urban districts examined 3rd grade scores on state tests in relation to students' historical attendance records from kindergarten and 1st grade. Applied Survey Research (2011) found that 64 percent of students who attended regularly in kindergarten and 1st grade (absent 5 percent or less of school days) received a score of proficient or better in reading at the end of 3rd grade. In comparison, only 17 percent of students who were chronically absent received a score of proficient or better. This finding is particularly alarming given that reading proficiency in 3rd grade is considered a critical milestone for long-term school success or failure. For example, researchers have found that students who do not read proficiently by the end of 3rd grade are four times more likely than their peers to drop out of school (Hernandez, 2011).

As soon as a child enters kindergarten, all families should receive information about the essential basic skills their child will learn in kindergarten. This information should emphasize that regular and repeated practice of skills such as phonemic awareness, phonics, and vocabulary in reading and one-to-one number correspondence in math is critical to set up their child for success. Even sporadic absences can cause their child to fall behind. You may need to help families understand that their children are no longer attending daycare and that ensuring regular attendance is one of the best things they can do to ensure their child's success in school and in life.

Students who are chronically absent have lower grade point averages and test scores. Controlling for student, classroom, school, and neighborhood characteristics, as well as past student performance, Gottfried (2010) found a positive relationship between the number of days the student was present at school and both GPA and standardized test results in the elementary and middle grades. This relationship was somewhat stronger for middle than elementary students and for mathematics than reading. A Georgia Department of Education report suggests that even a few days of missed school can make a difference on achievement outcomes. Based on attendance and state test data from a 2007 cohort of 9th graders, the report estimated that increasing average student attendance by just 3 percent (or

5 instructional days in a traditional 180-day school calendar) could have led to 10,000 more students passing the state reading test and 30,000 more students passing the state mathematics test (Barge, 2011). Students who reported missing three or more days of school in the month before testing for the National Assessment of Educational Progress (NAEP) scored more than a full grade level lower on the reading and math assessments than peers with no absences (Ginsberg, Chang, & Jordan, 2014).

Early absenteeism predicts later absenteeism. Multiple studies have found that children who are chronically absent in their earliest school years (preK through grade 1) continue to have attendance problems as they progress through school (Buehler, Tapogna, & Chang, 2012; Connolly & Olson, 2012; Ehrlich, Gwynne, Pareja, & Allensworth, 2013). For example, Ehrlich and colleagues (2013) found that students who were chronically absent in preschool were five times more likely to be chronically absent in 2nd grade than their peers, and that almost a third of students who were chronically absent in both preschool and kindergarten continued to have attendance problems by 2nd grade. A longitudinal study that followed students in Baltimore City Public Schools in Maryland from 6th grade through high school found that the 20 percent of students who missed the most days were cumulatively absent, on average, almost one full year (Baltimore Education Research Consortium, 2011).

Generally, as students accumulate missed instructional days throughout their school career, their risk for academic failure increases. Each successive year of chronic absenteeism is related to significant and compounded risk of reduced learning (Chang & Romero, 2008; Easton & Engelhard, 1982; Ehrlich et al., 2013). For example, in one study, students who were chronically absent in both kindergarten and 1st grade scored the lowest on 5th grade reading achievement tests—lower than students who were chronically absent in only one of these grades (Buehler et al., 2012).

Students with high levels of absenteeism are at greater risk for dropping out than peers with regular attendance. Studies have shown that students who eventually drop out of school are absent more often than other students and that absenteeism is predictive of dropout beginning as early as 1st grade (Alexander, Entwisle, & Horsey, 1997; Balfanz & Byrnes, 2012; Balfanz, Herzog, & Mac Iver, 2007; Hammond, Linton, Smink, & Drew, 2007; Neild, Balfanz, & Herzog, 2007; Rumberger & Thomas, 2000). In fact, research has consistently identified chronic absenteeism as one of the strongest predictors of dropping out of school—stronger even than suspensions, test scores, and being older than peers (Byrnes & Reyna, 2012).

Longitudinal outcomes illustrate just how much attendance in early grades influences graduation rates. A retrospective analysis of data from 790 students in Baltimore City Public Schools shows a clear and significant relationship between attendance in 1st grade and graduation outcomes. Students who eventually dropped out of school missed an average of 16 days in 1st grade, compared with graduates, who averaged about 10 absences. For each additional day that a student was absent in 1st grade, the likelihood of dropping out increased by about 5 percentage points (Alexander, Entwisle, & Horsey, 1997).

For students in middle and high school, changes in attendance can be as predictive of on-time graduation as test scores (Kieffer, Marinell, & Stephenson, 2011). A statewide analysis of attendance data in Utah found that students who are chronically absent during any year between 8th and 12th grade are 7.4 times more likely to drop out than students who regularly attend school (Utah Education Policy Center, 2012).

As Sheldon and Epstein (2004) conclude, "Studies of dropout show that leaving school is merely the culminating act of a long withdrawal process from school forecast by absenteeism in the early grades" (p. 40). The gradual process of disengagement is reflected in outcome variables such as chronic absenteeism and eventual dropping out of school. A lack of interest in school may lead to students being chronically absent as a part of the dropping-out process—they attend school less and less until they are faced with academic failure or decide to stop coming altogether.

Problems with Behavior and Social-Emotional Aspects of School

Students may act out due to frustration. Falling behind in their classes due to absenteeism can lead to a dangerous pattern of negative behavior and exclusion. Picture the following vicious cycle: A student acts out due to frustration with academic or social difficulties in classes. If the behavior is serious, it leads to exclusion from class and school activities. The student's absence leads to further frustration upon the student's return to class or school, which can then perpetuate the cycle of exclusion. In many cases, frustration can lead to more withdrawal and absences from school (Finn, 1989).

Students who are frequently absent from school experience fewer opportunities to build positive relationships with adults. School connectedness is one of the critical factors that has been identified as leading to success or failure in school (Fredericks, Blumenfeld, & Paris, 2004).

A defining feature of connectedness is the quality of a student's interactions and relationships with adult staff members. Students who are frequently absent may find it difficult to build meaningful connections with staff members. Furthermore, some staff may express frustration or even overt anger toward a student who is frequently absent, causing a further breakdown in the quality of that student's relationships.

In addition, effectively addressing absenteeism issues often requires a partnership between the student's parents and the school. When a student is frequently absent, it is common for school personnel to make judgments about the parents (e.g., "They just don't care about their child's education"), and parents may feel frustration toward the school (e.g., "They aren't addressing the problems that make my child want to stay home" or "They keep suspending my child and putting my job in jeopardy"). These judgments and adversarial relationships can make it increasingly difficult to help the student tackle an attendance problem.

Students who are chronically absent may not develop behavioral and social-emotional skills necessary for success in school and life. Students who are chronically absent tend to report a lower self-concept of their academic ability and lower levels of self-esteem in general than their peers who regularly attend school (Reid, 1982). The lag in academic performance that often results in frequent absenteeism can further affect a student's self-perception and increase the likelihood of greater disengagement from school (Griffin, 2002).

When students are absent to avoid aversive situations at school, such as conflict with peers or staff, bullying, academic difficulties, or other uncomfortable interactions, they may not develop necessary skills such as conflict resolution, resilience, and self-advocacy. They will learn over time to simply avoid discomfort by withdrawing and not attending school, work, or other uncomfortable situations.

Students may have difficulty establishing and maintaining positive peer relationships. Research has suggested that students who are chronically absent face increased alienation from classmates and peers (Gottfried, 2014; Reid, 1981). Friendships may shift when the student is frequently absent, as the student's friends seek out peers who are more consistently available. Peers may also resent picking up the slack for a student who is absent when there is a group project or partner work, or helping an absent student catch up when the student returns to school.

Negative Behaviors and Activities Outside School

Students exhibit higher rates of involvement in delinquent and other risk-taking behavior and are at increased risk for involvement in the criminal justice system. Chronic absenteeism is linked to increased crime and delinquency (Dalun et al., 2010; Farrington, 1996; Loeber & Farrington, 2000). Students who are chronically absent are also more likely to engage in risky behaviors, such as use of drugs and alcohol, early sexual experiences, and gang activity (Dryfoos, 1990; Garry, 1996; Hallfors et al., 2002; Henry & Huizinga, 2007).

Students who are frequently absent from school are also substantially more likely to experience negative outcomes later in life. For example, based on results from a longitudinal study of boys in South London, boys who were considered truant at age 14 were 2.5 times more likely to be convicted of a crime by age 50 compared with students who were not truant (Rocque, Jennings, Piquero, Ozkan, & Farrington, 2016).

Students may form detrimental habits and mindsets about dependability that can affect job performance. If students do not develop the habits of attending school and showing up on time every day when they are not seriously ill, they may be less likely to be at work regularly and on time when they enter the workforce. This lack of dependability can lead to serious negative outcomes, such as a lack of promotion despite one's talents and abilities or being fired. For example, a high school principal in Oregon explained to us that he tracked the job performance and attendance of recent graduates who entered the local job market. He found that students who had problematic attendance in high school continued to have problematic attendance in their jobs. Researchers have also found that adults who were frequently truant as teenagers tend to have poorer mental health outcomes, lower-paying jobs, and an increased likelihood of unemployment (Alexander et al., 1997; Hibbett, Fogelman, & Manor, 1990; Kane, 2006; Robins & Ratcliff, 1980).

How Irregular Attendance Negatively Affects the Class and the School

Just as students with irregular attendance can be negatively affected by their absenteeism, so too are teachers and other students, as well as the school as a whole. The next sections examine these extended effects.

Negative Effects on Teachers

Teachers lose valuable preparation and instructional time because of the need to deal with absences. When students are absent, many parents say, "Send home makeup work, and we will make sure she gets caught up." However, preparing this work requires significant time and effort if it is to provide a somewhat adequate level of instruction to make up for the missed class activities. The teacher also has to put in extra effort to track differing due dates for makeup work and ensure that the student is making sufficient progress after an absence. This is time that could be spent planning meaningful classroom activities.

When students are unwilling or unable to get themselves caught up outside the classroom and their parents can't help, the teacher is forced to spend class time helping those who were absent catch up with the rest of the class. In fact, numerous studies have found that when students are chronically absent, instruction for all students is slowed and a significant amount of instructional time is lost (Blazer, 2011; Chang & Jordan, 2011; Musser, 2011; Nauer, White, & Yerneni, 2008).

Classroom instructional activities are more difficult when students are frequently absent. Most educators will attest to the importance of building a trusting class community to facilitate learning. Because learning requires people to be vulnerable and admit to themselves and others that they do not know everything, a certain level of comfort and trust with peers and adults in the learning environment is essential. When students are frequently absent, it is difficult to build this kind of trusting community. Students may be reluctant to be vulnerable, make mistakes, and attempt to learn.

Furthermore, in classes that use partner and group activities, absences cause numerous difficulties. Teachers who do not have efficient procedures for regrouping students may struggle to place peers of absent students into new partnerships or groups without losing instructional time. Teachers may also experience difficulties with classroom climate, evidenced by such things as peers resenting having to take over work for their absent classmate, or struggles to maintain instructional momentum within groups.

Teachers can experience frustration and anxiety related to absenteeism. When students are frequently absent, the resulting teacher stress can contribute to a negative climate. Because teachers are concerned about the general progress of the class, student absences may lead to teacher frustration or anxiety. This situation may be especially prevalent in schools or districts where there is increased accountability or pressure for students to perform well on standardized tests, as the teacher may be concerned about how a student's absenteeism will adversely affect the class's learning and thus job performance reports.

Furthermore, as noted earlier, studies suggest that students who are chronically absent tend to exhibit greater frequencies of disruptive behavior (Gottfried, 2014), requiring teachers to spend more time and resources on behavior management and detracting from the time available to serve other students. When students with absenteeism issues also have behavioral issues, this situation may contribute to increased frustration toward the student, which leads to a further breakdown in positive relationships and student disengagement from school.

Negative Effects on Other Students

Classrooms with high rates of absenteeism may experience a lack of adequate academic growth for all students. When a teacher must spend significant class time reteaching the whole group or small groups, or providing individual instruction due to absences, the whole class may experience a significantly reduced pace of learning. Gottfried (2014, 2015) found that when chronically absent students do attend school, they often require significant remediation, slow the pace of instruction, and, in turn, reduce the opportunity for academic gains for others in the class. Musser (2011) similarly concluded that in schools with high rates of chronic absenteeism, learning outcomes for all students are affected.

Students may experience frustration or anxiety due to peers' absences. In partner and group activities, students who have to compensate or adjust for absent peers may experience frustration and resentment toward those peers and the teacher. They may also recognize that their own pace of learning has slowed because learning time is being taken to update absent students, which may also lead to resentment. Furthermore, when the absent student has corresponding behavioral difficulties, students may feel frustration or anxiety over their peer's acting-out behavior.

Peers may observe absenteeism and begin to question why they need to attend. We often hear educators express concerns that students' observation of frequent absences among their peers leads to a general devaluing of school and the importance of attendance. They fear that absenteeism can be contagious—the more some students are absent, the more others will also decide that attendance is optional.

Detrimental Effects for the School

Absenteeism affects levels of school funding in some states. State funding for schools is based on either attendance or student enrollment. In districts where funding is tied to attendance, chronic absenteeism costs money and decreases the educational resources available to all students (Smink & Reimer, 2005). For example, an analysis of the Houston Independent School District found a loss of approximately $22.3 million in funding for every 1 percent reduction in Average Daily Attendance across the district (Finck, 2015).

Negative effects of absenteeism may cause particular schools to be viewed as less desirable. When a school has lower test scores and GPAs, higher dropout rates, or other negative effects related to high rates of absenteeism, it may receive a lower score on ratings of schools. This lower rating can lead to decreased enrollment, less desirable applicants for jobs at the school, and corresponding negative effects such as state or federal sanctions.

Problems for Families, Community, and Society

It is hardly surprising that absenteeism has an effect on the people who are closest to and ultimately responsible for students—namely, parents. Siblings are also affected. Perhaps less obvious are the negative effects on the community and society in general. In the next sections we look at the effects on each of these groups.

Negative Effects on Parents

Many parents struggle to adjust their schedule or find adequate care for a student who is not in school. Providing supervision for a child who is not in school requires most parents to take time off from work or from doing other necessary activities, which can lead to increased parental stress and frustration with the student, with the school, or in general. For many parents, taking time off work is simply not an option, as they run the risk of losing their job. They may need to scramble to find an alternative caregiver or, in the worst-case scenario, simply leave their child unsupervised during an absence or suspension. Each of these situations can cause hardship on the family, especially when absences are frequent.

Frequent suspensions or absences may create adversarial relationships between the parents and school staff. Absences due to suspension can lead to adversarial relationships between parents and school staff.

Parents may wish to support the school but feel frustrated by its inability to handle school-based problems onsite. They may also be concerned about possible ramifications related to their job and feel the school is placing an undue burden on them by suspending the student.

When a student is absent to avoid school-related concerns (e.g., conflict and fighting, bullying, negative relationships with staff, or academic difficulties), adversarial relationships between parents and the school may occur if the parents feel the school is not doing everything possible to alleviate concerns. Or, if the school does appear to be doing everything possible, parents may feel frustration that the school is not equipped to support their child.

Negative Effects on Siblings

Excessive absenteeism tends to run in families. Barriers such as a lack of reliable transportation and other causes of absenteeism that affect one child will affect siblings similarly (Black, Seder, & Kekahio, 2014). Therefore, if one student has no reliable way to get to school, this same barrier will likely affect younger siblings. Children may also watch older siblings and adopt their school-related habits and attitudes. Furthermore, when students are chronically tardy or taken out of school early—for example, because of a doctor or dentist appointment or participation in a sporting event—parents will often drop off or pick up all their children at the same time, even if only one child is directly involved.

Teachers and other staff may exhibit biases toward siblings of a student with absenteeism or behavioral issues. If an older sibling has struggled with absenteeism, teachers may automatically expect that younger siblings will do the same and thus exhibit lower expectations for the younger students' success. Some teachers may struggle to build positive relationships with younger siblings who enter their class because they make negative assumptions from the outset, especially if the older sibling had behavioral issues. If this situation is common in a school, it should be addressed through staff development on the importance of viewing each child as an individual and holding high expectations regardless of family history; but it can also be addressed by putting effective prevention and intervention in place to address familial patterns of absenteeism.

Negative Effects on Communities and Society in General

Increased dropout rates have significant economic consequences. Because high rates of absenteeism are strongly related to students dropping out of school, any negative effects of dropouts on communities and society can be associated with chronic absence as well. For example, the estimated economic consequences of dropping out of school are immense—averaging close to $240,000 per dropout—as a result of lower tax contributions once the dropout reaches adulthood, greater reliance on government programs and assistance, and higher rates of criminal activity (Levin & Belfield, 2007; Maynard, Salas-Wright, & Vaughn, 2015; Rouse, 2007).

Communities pay the price for undesirable behaviors, criminal activity, and lack of job preparedness. Consider also the negative effects on the student that were discussed earlier in this chapter. If chronic absence is linked to crime and delinquency and students who are chronically absent are more likely to use drugs and alcohol, have early sexual experiences, and engage in gang activity, the costs to communities and society are immense. If students are less likely to develop the habits and attitudes that are essential for satisfactory job performance, they are more likely to place a burden on their communities later in life as they struggle to acquire and maintain a job.

■ ■ ■ ■ ■

Student attendance has wide-reaching implications for our students, our schools, and our communities. In this chapter we provided summaries of research on the prevalence of absenteeism in our schools and its negative effects. We also shared negative effects that, although not yet supported by research, have been described to us by countless educators around the United States as we have worked with them to tackle attendance issues in their schools. As you read the next chapters, consider which findings will be most relevant for convincing your staff, students, families, and community that improving attendance for all students must be a priority. This information can be useful in providing the rationale and foundation upon which to base your initiative to build a culture of regular school attendance.

Building an Effective Team

The procedures we present in this book assume that everyone in a school community has a stake in improving attendance and thus has a role to play in helping students and families achieve this goal. Rather than relegating the job to an attendance clerk or a counselor, this book highlights the importance of a team-led approach. In this chapter we describe how to build an effective team that will analyze attendance data and disseminate information and resources to all staff and other members of your school community. When everyone does a little to tackle the issue, schools find that the onus on any individual staff member is significantly reduced, cultural change begins to occur, and schoolwide attendance improves.

Determine What Team Will Work on Attendance Issues

Consider whether universal attendance issues can reasonably be addressed by a Positive Behavioral Intervention and Supports (PBIS) team, a Multi-tiered System of Support (MTSS) team, or some other existing team, or whether a new team should be formed. When a team is already well established and functions to tackle school priorities, it might be reasonable to add absenteeism to its responsibilities. This approach might also be feasible when the absenteeism problems are limited to a relatively small number of students (see Chapter 3 for information on tracking and analyzing attendance data). However, if existing teams are at or beyond their capacity with current responsibilities, or if absenteeism is pervasive, it may be necessary to form a task force within an existing team or an entirely new team. In the task force option, a subset of the larger team meets regularly to focus specifically on attendance issues. With either a task force or a new team, ensure that at least one member serves as a liaison with other behavior and academic teams to avoid competing efforts and duplicated work. Regardless of the team structure, it is important to ensure that attendance issues do not get pushed aside or receive insufficient time for analysis and planning in relation to the magnitude of your school's absenteeism problems.

As much as possible, the team should include members from across the school staff, including the following:

- In a larger school, at least one administrator (e.g., principal, assistant principal, dean); in a smaller school with only one administrator, a lead teacher or an interventionist
- Interventionists, especially those who deal with attendance or related issues (e.g., counselor, social worker, school psychologist, behavior interventionist)
- Several teachers, from both general education and special education
- School resource officer or campus security officer
- Attendance clerk or other classified staff member in charge of attendance data

Also consider including at least one student representative and one parent representative who will attend portions of meetings that require student and parent input but are not present during discussions of sensitive issues such as those involving individual students or staff members. When important policies or procedures are discussed, it may be beneficial to convene an advisory panel composed of students, parents, and community members. Some schools may opt to create or use an existing student advisory panel led by a staff member who is part of the attendance team.

In our work in schools across the United States, we have seen highly effective teams that succeeded in creating positive change, including significant reductions in office disciplinary referrals and suspensions, improved attendance, and improved staff morale and sense of efficacy. These teams have clear goals and objectives, meeting structures, and roles and responsibilities, and they continuously work to get all staff members on board with the initiative. We've also seen less effective teams that, because of unclear systems and structures, become bogged down on single issues with no hope of resolution, fall into endless cycles of brainstorming without follow-up, or get stuck venting about individual students who have a highly resistant problem. Some teams get sidetracked by tangential issues and never tackle their major priorities, and others end up resented and undermined by the rest of the staff because they are ineffective in playing the politics of implementation. The following sections provide clear steps to help you form and maintain a highly effective and productive attendance team.

Create Meeting Structures to Ensure Team Work Is Productive

How a team is structured can make a big difference in how effective and productive it is. Here are some specific guidelines for helping to ensure that the team will operate efficiently, gain support from the larger school community, and ultimately achieve its goals.

Assign Team Members as Staff Representatives

Part of the rationale for having team members from varied staff roles is to ensure that every staff member is represented. Once your team is formed, list each member and the staff group represented. See Figures 2.1 and 2.2 for examples of a team representation structure.

FIGURE 2.1 **Sample Attendance Team Organization for High School**

Team Member	Staff Members Represented by Team Member
Dean of students	Principal, assistant principals
Counselor	Counselors, social workers, school psychologist, behavior and academic interventionists
Special education teacher	Special education teachers, instructional assistants, occupational and speech therapist, ELD specialists
9th grade teacher	9th and 10th grade general education teachers
12th grade teacher	11th and 12th grade general education teachers
Office attendance secretary	Office administrative assistants, custodial and lunchroom staff
School resource officer	Campus security staff, nursing staff

FIGURE 2.2 **Sample Attendance Team Organization for K–5**

Team Member	Staff Members Represented by Team Member
Assistant principal	Principal, assistant principals, school psychologist, instructional coach, nursing staff
Social worker	Counselor, English language learner specialists, special education teachers, paraprofessionals
1st grade teacher	General education teachers and instructional assistants in grades K–2
4th grade teacher	General education teachers and instructional assistants in grades 3–5
Custodian	Office administrative assistants, custodial and lunchroom staff, "noon duty" supervisors

Each team member will periodically seek advice on the team's efforts from the staff members represented—for example, asking whether a proposed plan is feasible or other considerations need to be taken into account. When staff members have concerns that they would like to bring to the team, their representative is the logical starting place. For example, any instructional assistant or member of the custodial, cafeteria, or nursing staffs who has a concern related to absenteeism or the attendance team's efforts should be able to speak confidentially with the group's representative—often another classified staff member. This team member can then bring the concern to the attendance team.

Create a Regular Meeting Schedule

Most teams or task forces should plan to meet once a month; however, some will meet more frequently—once a week, for example—when absenteeism is a significant problem. Meetings should be long enough to ensure that the team can analyze schoolwide data, develop plans to address concerns, and allocate responsibilities for creating needed materials or guiding implementation. In many cases it may be beneficial to schedule a regular one-hour meeting throughout the school term and conduct a half- or full-day planning session once a quarter.

Create a Vision for the Attendance Team

Effective teams engage in the following actions (which we explain in detail in subsequent chapters):

- Meet on a regular schedule with specific goals and objectives;
- Administer and analyze data for decision making (Chapter 3);
- Plan schoolwide approaches (Chapters 4–9);
- Ensure that tiered systems of support are created and maintained (Chapters 10–11);
- As much as possible, create all materials needed for schoolwide and classroom implementation; and
- Provide ongoing communication on attendance data and team/school efforts with staff, students, and families.

It may be useful to list these actions on a chart that is displayed whenever the team meets, to remind members of the breadth and depth of what they should accomplish during meetings.

Assign Team Member Roles

Assigned roles keep meetings running smoothly and provide each team member with a position of authority and responsibility. Work with the team and consider the personal strengths of each member when assigning the following roles.

Chair. The chair is responsible for keeping the meeting focused on the agenda and ensuring that meeting norms and expectations are followed. This person prepares agendas and sends them to team members before the meeting and also provides periodic reminders to members to complete assigned action items. The chair should also work with the recorder to ensure that the team sets dates for starting and completing action items and follow-up tasks, and that personnel who will carry out the tasks are clearly identified. This role is best served by someone well respected by the staff who has good communication skills and who can be assertive in keeping meetings focused and productive.

Cochair. The cochair (who may also have other assigned responsibilities on the team) shares the duties of the chair and ensures that meetings run smoothly when the chair is not available. The cochair might be assigned to use a stopwatch to keep track of times for each agenda item and provide periodic warnings as the end time for each item nears. This attentiveness will help keep meetings focused on completing each task within the specified time.

Recorder. The recorder is responsible for taking notes on all meetings, with enough detail so that someone who was not present can understand the discussions that took place and any decisions made. Particular attention should be paid to recording outcomes of discussions and specifying dates and personnel responsible for any follow-up tasks. The recorder must be able to take clear notes (preferably typed or transcribed soon after the meeting) and summarize key points.

Materials manager. This team member keeps a paper-based and digital archive of all meeting agendas and notes, materials created for staff members, documents sent home to families, and other materials. Organizational skills are critical for this role.

Data coordinator. The data coordinator gathers any data requested by the team and may be responsible for preliminary analyses of data (e.g., identifying the percentage of the student body that is chronically absent). When data presentations are given to the staff or shared with families, the data coordinator prepares visuals or summaries to make the information easy to understand. This role is often filled by an interventionist or other staff member who has (or can be given) access to the schoolwide attendance system and other data management systems.

Keeper of the list. The keeper of the list redirects conversations when discussions begin to stray from the posted agenda and maintains a record of the divergent topics as possible items for future agendas. For example, if the team is discussing classroom-based systems for attendance motivation but gets sidetracked into a discussion about the need for more engaging classroom instruction, the keeper of the list can remind the team that the goal is to determine whether and how to propose classroom-based motivational systems to the teachers at the next staff meeting. The keeper of the list would write down "engaging classroom instruction as a way to boost attendance" in the list of topics to discuss at a subsequent meeting. At the end of the meeting, the team can decide which of the listed items they want to add to the next agenda.

Liaisons with other teams and stakeholders. Additional roles may be assigned to ensure that the attendance team communicates with and works in conjunction with other teams and stakeholders. For example, if a climate and safety team is planning to conduct a survey to assess student perceptions of respect, safety, and other climate variables, the liaison would be responsible for ensuring that the attendance team does not survey students in the same month. Although all team members will be responsible for matters such as equity and family engagement, other liaison roles might be assigned to ensure that these issues receive specific attention. Here are some possible additional liaison roles:

- **Equity and student liaison**—Monitors data and discussions related to inequities and advocates for and with students.

- **Family and community engagement liaison**—Encourages efforts to increase family and community involvement in attendance initiatives and serves as a conduit for bringing family and community concerns to the team. This person might have shared responsibilities with a family engagement team or have direct, regular contact with parent organizations such as the PTA or PTO.

- **MTSS liaison**—Ensures that the attendance team is working in conjunction with other systems of prevention and intervention in the school—for example, connects with the school psychologist for issues related to special education evaluation.

Create Meeting Norms or Expectations

Work with team members to create a set of meeting norms to increase productivity and effective collaboration. Identify four to six norms that will be posted and reviewed at the beginning of every meeting. As team members brainstorm possible norms, ask them to identify actions and qualities that helped previous teams function effectively as compared with behaviors and attitudes that led to breakdowns in communication or productivity. Here are some possible meeting norms:

- Start and end on time.

- Keep attention and conversation focused on the agreed-upon agenda items.

- Keep minutes for all meetings and distribute them promptly to the team and all staff.

- Identify specific tasks to be accomplished, including staff responsible and timelines, and include these tasks, staff, and timelines in all meeting minutes.

- Attend all meetings except when emergencies arise.

- Assume positive intent in all conversations, especially disagreements.
- Focus on problem solving, not venting.

Take the time to discuss and come to an agreement on the meeting norms the team will adopt. Ensure that all team members have a common understanding of how to implement the norms and agree that everyone on the team has a shared responsibility to help each other follow the norms (Schwarz, 2016).

Conduct Effective Team Meetings

With a well-crafted structure in place, the attendance team can begin its work. The following guidelines will help to ensure that meetings run smoothly and lead to the desired outcomes.

Use a Preplanned Agenda

Use or create a template for an agenda and minutes so that each meeting follows a standard protocol. For each section of the agenda, assign times to ensure that all items are addressed and the meeting stays within the allotted time. See Figure 2.3 for a sample template for a one-hour meeting.

When planning the agenda for each meeting, be reasonable about what the team can accomplish during the specified meeting time. If the agenda has too many tasks, determine which ones can be assigned to do outside the meeting time and which ones will need to be tabled until a subsequent meeting. If the team continually finds that there are too many priorities to tackle within the allocated meeting time and the magnitude of the school's attendance problems warrants additional efforts, it may be necessary to increase the frequency and duration of the meetings. For example, instead of one hour once a month, plan a half or full day of work time at the beginning of each quarter, with one-hour follow-up meetings once a month or every other week.

It is important to assign responsibilities for follow-up tasks. The agenda template should have a section that clearly outlines who is responsible for doing specific tasks and a date for completion. Whenever the team discusses an implementation step, ensure that the following questions are asked:

- What exactly is the product or action that needs to be accomplished? For example, are there materials to create? Are there additional data to gather? Does staff buy-in or feedback need to be solicited?

FIGURE 2.3   **Agenda and Minutes for a One-Hour Attendance Team Meeting**

Meeting Date and Time: _____

Members in Attendance:

❏ **Agenda and Reminder** about this meeting was sent out a week before. Date reminder was sent: _____
❏ **Start the meeting ON TIME.** Time started: _____
❏ **Review tasks from last meeting.** Report status of current tasks and discuss tasks that still need to be done. (10 min.)
❏ **Review potential next tasks and decisions to address.** (5 min.)
❏ **Discuss what needs to occur to make the next tasks and decisions happen.** (30 min.)
❏ **Write down who is going to do what and when that person will do it.**

	Who	Does What	When
1)			
2)			
3)			
4)			
5)			
6)			
7)			

❏ **Review** who is going to do what and when that person will do it. (5 min.)
❏ **Ask if any other items need to be addressed** or need to be on the agenda for the next meeting. (3 min.)
❏ **Document** how the information discussed will be shared with the entire faculty. (5 min.)
❏ **Debrief** how the team did with regard to following its ground rules. (2 min.)
❏ **Remind** people when the next meeting is.
   Next meeting is _____ at _____ in _____
                         (date)   (time)   (location)
❏ **Adjourn meeting** at scheduled time. Meeting adjourned:
_____

- Who will be responsible for completing the product or action? In some cases, this may be multiple team members, but assign one person to lead the efforts.
- When can the team expect the product or action to be completed?

At the end of each meeting, review the action items, who is going to do what, and a deadline for completion of each action item.

Ensure Effective Management of Materials

All discussions, decisions, documents, and other team efforts should be clearly documented and easily accessible. Team members should be able to quickly find information at any time, and it is important to keep organized records of all implementation steps for future teams and staff members. Although the recorder will be the primary person responsible for keeping these records, all members should share some responsibility for ensuring that accurate archival records are maintained. We recommend that documents be kept in different binders or file boxes that are easily accessible by any member of the team (e.g., kept in a file cabinet in the main office). Electronic records should be saved on a computer that is located away from the physical documents or in a cloud storage system, if available. Here is a list of documents to keep, organized in at least two notebooks:

Process Notebook (working documents)

- Team composition, representation of staff, responsibilities on team
- Meeting calendar
- Meeting agendas and minutes
- Data summaries
- Current priorities
- Presentations and communications with staff
- Communications with families and the community

Archival Notebook (finalized documents and evidence of implementation)

- Team purpose or vision and mission statement
- Schoolwide policies for attendance
- Lesson plans for teaching students about the importance of attendance
- Attendance orientation materials for new students

- Materials for teaching families and the community about the importance of attendance
- Implementation materials or records of actions taken to address attendance problems specific to the school (see Chapter 8 for tailored strategies to address schoolwide priorities)
- Descriptions of systems of identification and intervention for Tier 2 and 3 interventions (see Chapters 10 and 11 for early-stage interventions and how to implement MTSS to address attendance issues)

Also consider ways to keep the staff handbook and student-parent handbook updated with major changes to policies or procedures related to attendance. At least annually, plan to review existing materials and update the student-parent handbook. It may be useful to have staff members bring their handbooks to each staff meeting and update them with replacement pages as needed.

■ ■ ■ ■ ■

Strategies described in this chapter lay the groundwork that will ensure that your team can work effectively together and with the broader school community to tackle attendance issues. The remaining chapters describe a range of strategies that your team can evaluate to determine which ones will have the greatest influence on your students, parents, staff, and community. Periodically evaluate whether your team is functioning as effectively as possible, and return to the tasks in this chapter to revitalize your team processes and procedures as needed.

■ ■ ■ ■ ■

Summary of Tasks for Building an Effective Team

Use the following outline as a quick reminder of the tasks involved in building and maintaining an effective team.

Establish a team to work on attendance issues.

- Assign responsibilities to an existing team or to a task force that is a subset of an existing team, or form a new team.

Create meeting structures to ensure that the team's work is productive.

- Select team members to represent staff groups.
- Ensure all certified and classified staff are represented by a member of the team.
- Determine how and when to communicate who the representatives are, their roles and responsibilities, and which staff members each person represents to the whole staff.
- Establish a schedule for regular meetings and place meeting dates on the calendar for the year.
- Create a vision for the attendance team and post related actions on a chart to display when the team meets.
- Assign team member roles for team meetings.
- Agree on four to six norms or expectations for meetings.

Conduct effective team meetings.

- Follow a preplanned agenda.
- Assign responsibilities for all follow-up tasks.
- Ensure effective materials management, including the following:
  - Working documents
  - Finalized documents and evidence of implementation
  - Updates to staff and student-parent handbooks

3

Creating Systems to Regularly Collect Data and Set Priorities

Jake Alabiso is the school psychologist at Barnes Elementary in Kelso, Washington, one of the schools that we have had the privilege to work with. He gave us the following account of the start of the school's attendance initiative:

> For years, the staff knew we had an attendance problem, but we failed to address the issue systematically. The reasons for this were threefold: (1) a lack of knowledge, (2) a mistaken belief that effecting meaningful change was not possible for what we thought to be primarily a home-based problem, and (3) the lack of accessible data. We plugged along for years with individual teachers and our attendance clerk occasionally lamenting our attendance issues but never developing any momentum to tackle the problem.
>
> In March 2014, all of this changed. We attended a conference where several of our PBIS team members attended Jessica Sprick's presentation on attendance. It struck a very strong chord with our team. We walked away armed with new vocabulary, data, research, and most important, hope that we could improve our schoolwide attendance rate. The aha moment came when the teachers roughly tabulated the attendance data for their individual classrooms. They were completely blown away by how much school their students were missing.

Jake's statement emphasizes the importance of good data in any initiative. To effectively intervene with any problem, you have to recognize that there *is* a problem. Then you must determine its magnitude and potential causes before a plan of action can be put in place. And it all requires data.

In this chapter we clarify definitions and methods for collecting data that you can use to identify schoolwide rates of problematic absenteeism as well as to identify individual students who require support. We also provide examples of data that you can collect to help determine priorities for prevention and intervention in your school and provide suggestions for when to collect different types of attendance data throughout the chapter.

The procedures may seem complicated, but your school or district likely has an attendance clerk who will have some knowledge about how to pull data from your school information system. If your attendance clerk is not familiar with how to compile the recommended reports, contact the information system operators and request information on how to gather necessary data.

Understand Commonly Used Metrics

Most schools currently collect data on truancy and Average Daily Attendance (ADA). Although these data are useful, it is important to recognize that relying on them alone can be misleading about the extent of a school's absenteeism problems.

The term *truancy* typically describes absences that occur without parent permission. These absences are important to track given their relationship to dropping out, delinquency, and other at-risk factors, and some evidence indicates that unexcused absences are associated with the strongest negative effects, such as academic failure (Gottfried, 2009). However, it is important to recognize that unexcused absences are not the only problematic type of absence. An overreliance on truancy data may cause a school to overlook other students whose attendance puts them at risk of disengagement and school failure. A student may experience negative effects of absenteeism (as described in Chapter 1) regardless of whether absences are unexcused or excused. Warning systems that look only at truancy often fail to catch a large number of students who exhibit problematic patterns of attendance, especially those that occur in elementary school, where the majority of absences are excused. Consider the following example of what can occur when a school looks only at truancy data.

Jeremiah was a 7th grader who was referred for Tier 3 supports due to failure across all his classes. When our intervention team examined his course records, it quickly became clear that he had patterns of excessive absenteeism (e.g., averaging about two or three days a week), but his attendance was never flagged as a problem because the school was looking at truancy and Jeremiah's absences were excused. He was triggered as needing support only when his course failures reflected the fact that he was rarely in class. As our team intervened to address Jeremiah's failing grades, one of the first things we knew we had to tackle was the pattern of severe chronic absence, but that effort had to start with getting his mom on board. Jeremiah would complain of colds and headaches to get out of coming to school, so we worked with his mother to implement a plan that required a doctor's visit or approval from the school nurse before Jeremiah's mom would allow him to stay home. As Jeremiah's attendance improved and we worked to address other issues like anxiety that were causing the absenteeism, Jeremiah's work completion, test scores, and grades also improved.

Average Daily Attendance is tracked in many schools, and in some states, it is a partial funding mechanism—the higher the ADA, the more funding the school receives. Average Daily Attendance is a measure of the average percentage of students in the student body who are present each day across the school year. In a school with a 92 percent ADA rate, for example, an average of 92 percent of the students are present each day. As a whole-school measure, ADA can be useful for getting a broad picture of the school's rate of attendance and setting whole-school goals for improvement (e.g., "We had an ADA of 92 percent last month; let's strive for 94 percent this month!"). However, ADA provides no information about individual students whose attendance contributes positively or negatively to the whole-school percentage. Even a school with an ADA of 95, which is often viewed as a good schoolwide rate, may have a significant number of students highly at risk of negative effects of absenteeism like academic difficulties and eventual dropout due to problematic attendance. This situation can occur when the majority of students have very good attendance and a smaller, significant number of students have poor attendance.

Truancy and ADA are important metrics for the attendance team to monitor. However, these metrics should be evaluated in conjunction with individualized, more specific metrics, as described in the next section.

Regularly Monitor Individualized Metrics and ADA

In the last 20 years, researchers and school professionals have attempted to determine critical thresholds, or red flags, that indicate when a student's absenteeism could be viewed as highly problematic and a likely route to failure and dropping out of school. The following individualized metrics—which should be calculated using a combination of unexcused absences, excused absences, and suspensions—have emerged as critical indicators:

- **Regular Attendance:** Absent 5 percent or less
- **At-Risk Attendance:** Absent 5.1–9.9 percent
- **Chronic Absence:** Absent 10 percent or more
- **Severe Chronic Absence:** Absent 20 percent or more

Here we describe the categories of Chronic Absence and Regular Attendance because Chronic Absence is the critical red flag for intervention, and Regular Attendance is the goal for every student.

Chronic Absence is defined as missing 10 percent or more of school days for any reason, including unexcused absences, excused absences, and suspensions. Note that in some schools, suspensions are considered excused absences and thus are also included when a district or school defines Chronic Absence as a measure of excused and unexcused absences.

This metric has emerged as the point at which absenteeism is strongly associated with negative outcomes such as failing a course and dropping out. In 2010, Sparks summarized the emerging research trends, stating, "A growing consensus of research points to chronic absence . . . as one of the strongest and most overlooked indicators of a student's risk of becoming disengaged, failing courses, and eventually dropping out of school" (p. 1). Since that time, an exponential increase in research has indicated a relationship between chronic absence and negative student outcomes. Therefore, along with a growing number of education experts, state departments of education, and federal sources, we recommend analyzing Chronic Absence data and using this metric as a measure of school effectiveness.

Regular Attendance is a related metric and is defined as missing 5 percent or fewer school days for any reason, including unexcused absences, excused absences, and suspension. Just as Chronic Absence is viewed as a critical point where negative effects are likely, Regular Attendance is viewed as a critical point where a school may assume that the student is unlikely to suffer negative effects related to absenteeism. Therefore, if a student attends school regularly but exhibits signs of disengagement, academic failure, or other concerns, the school can likely rule out absenteeism as the cause of these negative patterns. The goal is that every student regularly attend school, missing no more than 5 percent of days in the school year.

In between Regular Attendance and Chronic Absence is the *At-Risk Attendance* category, in which a student may or may not suffer negative effects of absenteeism but should be carefully monitored. For students in this category, schools should implement early-stage interventions to try to prevent further problems with absenteeism and increasingly intensive interventions as the problems persist.

Severe Chronic Absence, defined as missing 20 percent or more of school days, can be viewed as an extreme level of chronic absenteeism that warrants immediate intervention. Without support and intervention, most students in this category are on a predictable path toward school failure. Note that we typically recommend that your schoolwide data only report chronic absence (10 percent or more), as students in the Severe Chronic Absence category are included in the Chronic Absence category. If you report schoolwide data with Severe broken out, it risks singling out students because (we hope) relatively few students are in this extreme. In addition, there is some risk that parents and students in the Chronic Absence category will minimize their own level of risk since these students are not "Severe." It is important for the school to calculate which students fall in the Severe Chronic Absence category, however, as these students warrant an additional level of concern and attention by school personnel.

When we began our work to help schools improve their attendance, the metric of Chronic Absence was relatively new and largely unknown to most educational professionals. It was revealing to watch participants' faces at conferences and district trainings when we talked about the importance of expanding beyond data related to truancy and ADA. Many participants came to sessions seeking answers for intervention with individual students who had 60, 90, or 100 days of absence. Because of school ADA percentages in the low or mid-90s and low rates of truancy, most educators thought that their schoolwide attendance wasn't that bad, but after learning the metrics of Regular Attendance and Chronic Absence, they quickly realized that the magnitude of the problem stretched far beyond individual students. It was quite common for participants to pull attendance data during lunch break and return to the session with ashen faces—realizing their schools have a high percentage of students chronically absent. Expanding beyond truancy and ADA data gives schools a fuller picture of how attendance is positively or negatively affecting them. This shift can then help schools determine how much time and energy to place on improving student attendance through a multitiered model.

View Attendance Metrics Within a Continuum

Note that although the categories of Regular Attendance, At-Risk Attendance, Chronic Absence, and Severe Chronic Absence are defined according to a specific percentage of days present or absent for the sake of clarity, we recommend thinking about students' attendance as a continuum that has increasing levels of risk associated with increased levels of absenteeism (see the thermometer in Figure 3.1). In reality, there is little difference between a student who has missed 9.5 percent of the school year and one who has missed 10 percent. Both students may need similar levels of support, even though one is defined as At-Risk and the other is in the Chronic Absence category.

Conceptualize Percentages Versus Number of Days

The definition of Chronic Absence uses a percentage, rather than number of days, to ensure that schools do not wait to intervene until a student has reached a certain number of days absent (e.g., 10 days or 18 days). The

FIGURE 3.1 **A Continuum of Risk**

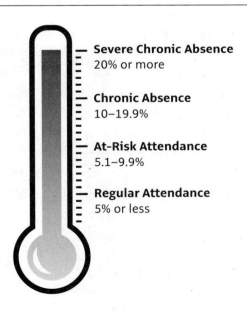

Severe Chronic Absence
20% or more

Chronic Absence
10–19.9%

At-Risk Attendance
5.1–9.9%

Regular Attendance
5% or less

percentage ensures that whenever data are analyzed during the school year, a school can identify students who are chronically absent, at risk, and regularly present at that particular point in the year. For example, a student would be considered chronically absent across the whole school year when he misses 10 percent of days, or 18 days in a 180-day school year. However, a school should not wait until the end of the year to determine that this student has a problematic attendance rate. If the student misses 10 percent in the first 20 days—that is, misses 2 or more days—intervention may be warranted. At the least, the school should carefully observe the student's attendance across the next 20 days. What is important to remember is that if the student misses an average of 2 or more days a month according to a typical school calendar (180 days), that student is considered chronically absent. If your school operates on a different school calendar (e.g., four-day weeks or a shortened or lengthened school year), calculate the attendance percentages accordingly.

Also remember and emphasize the goal that you want *every* student to be regularly present (missing no more than 5 percent of days). This means that each student should miss no more than an average of 1 day per month in a typical 180-day school year.

For the first two months of the school year, collect and analyze data at least once a month to trigger early prevention and intervention efforts. After that, collect and analyze data on attendance rates at least once every two months.

Calculate the Schoolwide Rate for Each Individualized Metric from the Start of School

At each point when attendance data are collected and analyzed, calculate the percentage of students who fit into each attendance category since the start of the school year. If you are uncertain whether your attendance system will allow you to pull Chronic Absence data and other individualized metrics, contact your district data coordinator or the developer of the management system. Because more school districts and states are requiring these data, many management system developers may be willing to build in this feature if it is not already available.

If your attendance system does not allow you to enter the percentage of days present or absent and filter accordingly, manually calculate each category. Figure 3.2 provides an example of how to manually calculate the percentage of students in the Regular Attendance category. Follow the same procedure to calculate the percentage of students in the At-Risk Attendance,

FIGURE 3.2 **Calculating the Percentage of Students in the Regular Attendance Category from the Start of School**

General Procedure	Example in a School of 500 Students
1. Calculate the number of days that equals 5 percent of the school year to date.	1. It is Day 80 of the school year. Five percent of 80 days is 4 days, so any student with 4 or fewer days absent since the start of school would be considered to have regular attendance.
2. Print a list of students who have been absent that number of days or fewer during the specified time period. Include all absences—unexcused, excused, and suspension.	2. The team prints a list of all students who have had 4 or fewer days of absence since the start of school.
3. Divide the number of students with regular attendance (the number of students identified in Step 2) by the number of enrolled students. Then multiply by 100 to get the percentage of students in the Regular Attendance category.	3. The team counts 279 students with 4 or fewer days of absence and divides 279 by the number of enrolled students (500). After multiplying by 100, the team sees that 55.8 percent of the student body is in the Regular Attendance category.

Note: The procedure does not take into account students who arrive after Day 1 of the school year (e.g., if a student arrives on Day 20 of school, her percentage will be different than the percentage for students who have been in school since Day 1). Attendance for these students may need to be calculated individually and then factored into the percentage for each category.

Chronic Absence, and Severe Chronic Absence categories. Adjust the percentages and number of days as needed (e.g., for At-Risk, calculate the number of days that equal 5 to 10 percent of days during the specified time period; for Chronic Absence, calculate the number of days that equal 10 percent of days during the specified time period).

 Sunrise Middle School Scenario

Note: The following school scenario will continue throughout this and the next chapter.

The staff at Sunrise Middle School thought they had minimal problems with attendance, as the school met the district's goal of 95 percent ADA at the end of the school year. After learning about the metrics of Chronic Absence and Regular Attendance, Sunrise staff members were shocked to learn that 105 students out of 700 enrolled had more than 18 absences, which meant that 15 percent of the student body was chronically absent and in the red zone of risk. Another 140 students had between 10 to 17 absences, placing 20 percent of the student body in the yellow zone (At-Risk category); and only 455 students, or 65 percent of the student body, were in the green zone (Regular Attendance category). Sunrise staff members now knew they had a schoolwide problem with absenteeism despite their 95 percent ADA rate. This information provided the catalyst for action.

Calculate the Schoolwide Rate for Each Individualized Metric from the Previous Data Point

In addition to calculating the rates of Regular Attendance, At-Risk Attendance, Chronic Absence, and Severe Chronic Absence from the start of the school year to the current date, calculate the rates for a smaller snapshot in time, looking at attendance from the previous data point to the current date. Looking at the data in these different ways allows the team to see overall trends as well as any changes across time. For example, if the team analyzed attendance data on Day 40 and it is now Day 80, look at the percentage of the student body in each of the categories from Day 1 to Day 80, and also from Day 41 to Day 80. Looking at the data from the previous data point will make it easier to see trends, both positive and negative. For example, if only 5 percent of students were chronically absent in the first two months of school, but the number jumps to 20 percent of students in months three and four, this spike in absenteeism will be more apparent when looking at the data for only months three and four.

⊘ **Sunrise Middle School Scenario** After identifying the magnitude of its attendance problem, Sunrise formed an attendance team whose responsibilities would include monitoring attendance data, determining priorities for improvement, and creating a schoolwide action plan. The team was a task force consisting of a subset of the school's PBIS team, and some other staff members also joined (e.g., the attendance clerk and a social worker). They began in the fall with significant efforts to increase awareness among students and families of the importance of attendance, and they initiated several classroom and schoolwide motivational systems. (These strategies will be described in detail in subsequent chapters.) The team carefully monitored the attendance data to identify trends. During the first two months of school, Sunrise's universal prevention efforts appeared to be making a difference for the majority of students. Only 5 percent of students fell into the Chronic Absence category, and 12 percent in the At-Risk Attendance category, representing a significant improvement from the previous year. Sunrise's ADA also improved to 96.2 percent over the previous year's 95 percent. The team shared the data with staff, students, and families to celebrate their success and push for additional improvements.

However, when Sunrise's attendance team looked at the data again at the end of the fourth month, they noticed a troublesome trend. By analyzing the data from the start of school (Day 1 to Day 80), the data still looked fairly good, with only slight increases in the percentages for At-Risk Attendance and Chronic Absence. However, when the team broke down the data and analyzed it from the previous data point (Day 41 to Day 80), they saw that many more students exhibited problematic attendance patterns in the third and fourth month of school than in the first two months. For example, Jacob had one absence throughout August and September but then had six absences in October and November. This student's overall rate placed him in the At-Risk category but looking at the data for months three and four placed him in the Chronic Absence category. The team recognized that they would need to undertake additional work to understand and address causes of absenteeism in their school.

This example shows the importance of data so that schools can celebrate successes but also begin to delve deeper and work for continuous improvement. It also demonstrates the importance of monitoring data to detect problematic trends as soon as possible.

Determine the Average Daily Attendance Rate

Monitor the school's Average Daily Attendance rate at each data point. This metric is calculated by determining the percentage of the student body in attendance each day and finding the average of these percentages across the course of the year. Most attendance systems have a report that will automatically calculate this rate. Determine the ADA from the start of the school year to the current date as well as the ADA from the last data point to the present. This metric can be used to monitor the overall health of your school's attendance as well as to set schoolwide goals and reward staff and students for improvements.

Periodically Analyze Additional Data to Determine Trends and Causes

The previous sections described the data that you should collect at least once every two months—Regular Attendance, At-Risk Attendance, Chronic Absence, Severe Chronic Absence, and ADA. The following data-collection activities can be done less frequently (e.g., once or twice a year) to identify trends and causes of absenteeism for large numbers of students in your school.

Filter Data to Determine Trends in Absenteeism

Many universal prevention efforts will be similar across all schools and districts. For example, classroom motivational systems (described in Chapter 5) can be effective with any student population, and the procedures for implementation remain largely the same. However, some universal systems will be specific to the causes of absenteeism that are common in a particular school and community. For example, the causes of absenteeism for students in a rural school in the Midwest may be different from those for students in an urban school on the East or West Coast. Analyze Chronic Absence data to look for patterns that may indicate a common cause of absenteeism for large numbers of students in your school. Identifying these patterns may clarify common causes of absenteeism, or they may indicate that you will need to collect more data through surveys, focus groups, or other methods. (Chapter 8 provides information on how to implement tailored strategies to address any of the common causes of absenteeism you identify.)

Demographic trends. Filter demographic data for students in the Chronic Absence and Severe Chronic Absence categories to see if any noticeable trends emerge. Consider the percentage of students with attendance problems who fall into the following groups:

- Are on free and reduced lunch
- Are in specific racial or ethnic groups
- Have an identified disability
- Have a chronic health condition
- Have been identified as requiring academic or behavioral support

Time-of-year trends. Break down Chronic Absence and ADA data by month and week to see if attendance is much better or much worse at particular times of year—for example, around breaks. The following example relates how a district broke down attendance data by time of year and identified a surprising trend that changed the nature of its universal prevention approach.

A district in Illinois broke down its Chronic Absence data by month and was surprised to find significantly higher rates of chronic absenteeism in the first month of school. The district initially thought that perhaps students and families were having difficulties getting back into the habit of going to school each day or that families were extending their summer vacations. It considered ways to address these issues through parent and student education and motivational systems. However, when the district further broke down the data, it found that only particular schools were having significant absenteeism problems in the first month of school. After asking students and families about this trend, the district realized that the schools with absenteeism problems did not have air conditioning and students were simply too hot to be motivated to come to school and learn each day. The district's universal prevention efforts needed to involve improving the cooling systems in these schools. Without these data, the district would have gone to great lengths to intervene with an entirely irrelevant approach.

Other trends. Periodically experiment with other ways to filter and analyze your ADA, truancy, and Chronic Absence data to see if additional trends emerge. Here are some possibilities:

- By day of the week
- By time of day
- By staff member (*Note:* These data should be viewed and discussed only by administrative personnel.)
- By school (at the district level)
- By neighborhood of residence or bus and walking zones
- By category of the absence—excused, unexcused, or suspension

Gather Additional Data to Determine Universal Priorities

It may be useful or necessary to gather additional data to help you better understand what is contributing to a particular absenteeism trend. You can collect these data through a variety of methods, such as a student or parent survey, focus groups of students or parents, or anecdotal notes kept by teachers on each reported cause of absence when students are missing from class.

Anonymous student survey. Figure 3.3 provides an example of an anonymous student survey that can be used to determine common causes

FIGURE 3.3 **Anonymous Student Survey on Causes of Absenteeism**

Approximately how many days have you been absent this year? (Circle one.)

| 0–1 | 2–5 | 6–9 | 10–17 | 18+ |

Indicate how often the following reasons contributed to your absences.	Never	Once	More than once
I was seriously ill.			
I had a cold, headache, toothache, or other minor or moderate illness.			
I was tired and needed to sleep.			
I had a doctor or dentist appointment.			
I felt anxious or depressed.			
I missed the bus.			
I had no transportation to school.			
It was not safe to walk to school.			
Weather made it too cold or too hot to walk.			
I had hygiene reasons (e.g., no clean clothes, no deodorant, felt dirty).			
I had to work.			
I had to take care of younger siblings or other family members.			
I didn't think it would matter if I was absent.			
I didn't think adults at school would notice or care that I was absent.			
I didn't think my peers at school would notice or care that I was absent.			
I didn't think my parents would notice or care that I was absent.			
I did not complete homework or assignments.			
I was not prepared for a test.			
I did not understand the work or expectations in class and didn't want to go.			

(continued)

FIGURE 3.3 **(continued)**

Indicate how often the following reasons contributed to your absences.	Never	Once	More than once
My classes were boring.			
I was having a conflict with peers.			
I was being teased or bullied.			
I was having trouble with a teacher or staff member.			
I was hanging out with friends outside school.			
I was spending time with my parent or guardian.			
I was using technology (video games, computer, cell phone) I can't use at school.			
I was doing things I wouldn't want to report to the school or my parents.			
I was competing or participating in a sport or activity unrelated to school.			
I was competing or participating in a school-sponsored sport or activity.			

of absenteeism. We recommend you use this survey at the end of a school year to set priorities for the following year, or you could administer it to students at the beginning of the year to ask about their experiences with absenteeism in the previous year. Tailor your survey for the appropriate time of year, age group, and specific factors that may contribute to absenteeism in your community. For primary students, the survey could be reworded and delivered to parents rather than students. Tool 9 in the Grad Nation Community Guidebook (guidebook.americaspromise.org), an online resource for reducing absenteeism and truancy, provides another survey example that examines reasons for tardiness and skipping classes (Balfanz, Fox, Bridgeland, & Bruce, 2013).

Sunrise Middle School Scenario The team at Sunrise decided to implement an anonymous survey to identify causes of absenteeism in the school. When the team analyzed their data, they found that a significant percentage of the student body indicated that they missed school because of serious, moderate, or minor illness. They also learned that many students missed school because they were having trouble with a teacher or staff member. When the team presented these results to the whole staff, the staff agreed that illness was a major factor causing student absences and that the start of cold and flu season might account for some of the spike in attendance problems in October and November. However, they were surprised that many students indicated they were having trouble with a teacher or staff member. The staff felt they had built great, positive relationships with students and were dismayed to find that a significant number of students would miss school because of poor relationships or conflicts with a teacher. The team knew it would have to do some work around addressing illness, but they felt they needed more information before proceeding with the issue of staff-student relationships. They decided to convene a focus group.

Focus groups. When data from other sources (e.g., filtered trends, surveys) point to a trend but the causes are not clear or well known, arrange a focus group to gather more information. For example, if you discover that students are absent far more frequently on Tuesdays than on any other day of the week and your team does not have a clear sense of why this is occurring, convene a focus group of students to help you understand the causes.

✓ **Sunrise Middle School Scenario** During the focus groups with randomly selected groups of students, team members found out that students were troubled by teachers' excessive sarcasm. Students said things like, "We know they are trying to be funny, but they make fun of us, and it's really hurtful. It makes me not want to go to that class." The team had students compile lists of statements made by teachers without listing teacher names or singling out specific teachers or students, and they presented the information to the whole staff. When teachers read the lists of statements, many of them ended up in tears because they had not realized how caustic and biting their statements had become. This simple act of awareness led to a change in teacher and staff behavior and concerted efforts to avoid sarcasm and build more positive relationships with students. In subsequent follow-ups, the student body indicated that the school was a much more positive and welcoming place to be.

Anecdotal teacher notes. For one month, have teachers take notes of the anecdotal reasons that students give for being absent. Compile the reasons and use this information to identify common causes.

One educational service district found that there were three main reasons that students were missing school, one of which was frequent medical and dental appointments. Identifying this as a priority allowed the schools to move forward with greater clarity as to what strategies they would need to put in place to tackle issues that were specific to their schools. For example, the schools increased communication and messaging with local medical and dental offices about scheduling appointments before or after school hours or varying appointment times, and they worked with parents to help prevent medical and dental problems that might result in appointments during school hours (e.g., providing toothpaste and toothbrushes to families in need, providing tips on dental health, linking students without dental care to preventive clinical care and insurance providers).

Chapter 8 provides information on how to tailor strategies for addressing absenteeism based on trends that are specific to your school and that emerge from surveys, focus groups, and other data-collection efforts.

Determine Priorities for Universal Prevention Based on Data

Use collected data to determine when and how much emphasis to place on universal prevention and to identify causes of absenteeism for large numbers of students. Use the following recommendations to guide your data-based decision making.

Use a Multitiered System Model to Determine Intensity of Universal Prevention

Some universal prevention efforts for absenteeism are probably warranted in all schools. However, their number and intensity depend on the magnitude of attendance problems in your school. In a multitiered system of support model, Tier 1 procedures are universal practices delivered to every student through schoolwide or classwide approaches. Figure 3.4 depicts the three-tiered MTSS triangle and the percentages of students who should fall into each tier when a school is providing effective levels of universal prevention and intervention. The general idea is that the universal systems in your school should be robust enough to help the majority of your students (80 to 90 percent) do the right thing without requiring individu-

FIGURE 3.4 **Multitiered System of Support Applied to Absenteeism**

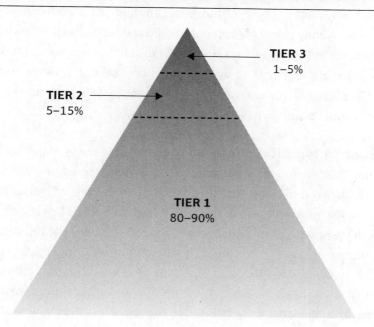

alized supports. Universal prevention efforts for attendance include things like creating awareness among staff, students, and families about the importance of attendance; implementing classwide and schoolwide motivational systems; and implementing tailored approaches that address issues particular to your school. (Strategies for universal prevention are described in Chapters 5 through 9). If fewer than 80 to 90 percent of your students are in the Regular Attendance category (missing no more than 5 percent of school days), plan to increase universal prevention efforts.

Note that if your school has significant challenges with absenteeism across the student body, you will need to invest additional time, effort, and personnel to design and implement universal systems. What another school might implement as a Tier 2 or Tier 3 approach could end up being an effective universal strategy for a school with more widespread absenteeism problems. For example, one school might identify a small group of students who have asthma and require targeted or individualized intervention at Tier 2 or 3, but a school with a large percentage of students with asthma would implement asthma-prevention procedures schoolwide.

Instill Values at the Elementary Level

Even if relatively few students struggle with attendance and few if any of the universal strategies recommended in this book have been implemented in your school, consider how to instill the value and habit of regular attendance in your students before they enter middle school. Attendance rates typically get steadily worse throughout middle and high school. Check Chronic Absence rates at the middle school and high school your school feeds into. If these rates are higher than at the elementary school, provide additional information for students and families in elementary school about the importance of school attendance (see Chapters 6 and 7).

✓ **Sunrise Middle School Scenario** Using the guideline of 80 to 90 percent of students in the Regular Attendance category using Tier 1 procedures, Sunrise staff knew that they needed to work at a universal level to help improve the attendance of the entire student body. They began at the start of the year with efforts to increase awareness about the importance of attendance and with class and schoolwide motivational systems (as described in Chapters 4 through 7). As the year went on, the team used data from the anonymous survey, focus groups, and other sources to identify universal strategies that were tailored to the specific causes of absenteeism in the school (see Chapter 8 for more on tailored strategies).

Use Red Flags to Trigger Intervention

Before the start of the school year, identify students with 10 percent or more absences in the previous school year and plan to start the year with increased supports for these students. At each subsequent data collection point, identify the individual students who fall into the At-Risk Attendance, Chronic Absence, and Severe Chronic Absence categories, and refer them as appropriate to an intervention planning team (e.g., student support team) or other personnel who can plan and provide intervention support. Pay particular attention to the following red flags:

- **Two or more absences in the first 20 days of school.** If a student is well connected with staff and students, has no history of chronic absence or other school difficulties, and has a legitimate reason for the absences, simply monitor whether the student's attendance improves in the next month. If the negative trend continues, intervene. If, however, a student has exhibited academic or behavioral difficulties or has a history of struggles in school, provide immediate early intervention (see Chapters 10 and 11 for intervention procedures and strategies).

- **Increasing frequency of absenteeism, especially in high school.** Increased frequency of absenteeism is often an indicator of some negative change for the student, and it is a clear sign of disengagement and the possibility of dropping out for older students. The Baltimore Education Research Consortium found that among students who dropped out in 2009, absenteeism increased steadily over the three years before they left while remaining steady for students who graduated (Mac Iver, 2010).

- **Any student in the Chronic Absence or Severe Chronic Absence category.**

- **Any student who has consistently been in the At-Risk Attendance category for an extended period.** If a student has a pattern of at-risk attendance across a period of three or more months (e.g., each month, the student has at-risk attendance), begin the process of intervention (see Chapter 10) to ensure this pattern does not continue or worsen.

Chapter 10 provides suggestions for early-stage interventions you can try when a student is first identified as having an absenteeism problem. Chapter 11 provides guidance on how to implement a cause-based or function-based approach for individuals with ongoing and resistant attendance concerns.

◼ ◼ ◼ ◼ ◼

Good work in schools starts with good data, and attendance data are an important tool to guide school improvement efforts. Now that you are collecting and analyzing attendance data regularly, the fun work of strategy implementation begins. Chapters 4 through 9 provide a range of universal strategies that you can use to inform, motivate, and reduce barriers to attendance throughout the school community. In discussing these universal strategies, one school practitioner informed us that "this work is the most gratifying work I've done in over 20 years in the field, and it has so much power to make a difference."

■ ■ ■ ■ ■

Summary of Tasks for Creating Systems to Collect Data and Set Priorities

Use the following outline as a quick reminder of the tasks involved in creating systems to regularly collect data and set priorities.

Regularly monitor rates for Regular Attendance, At-Risk Attendance, Chronic Absence, Severe Chronic Absence, and ADA.

- Indicate dates when the team will review these data (at least every two months).

Periodically analyze additional data to determine trends and causes.

- Indicate how you will filter data (e.g., percent of students in different demographic categories, time of year) or collect additional data (e.g., survey, focus group).
- Indicate when these data will be analyzed.

Regularly use red flags to trigger intervention.

- Indicate dates when the team will use red flags to identify students who require intervention.
- Indicate what red flags will trigger intervention.
- Clarify procedures for referring students who meet red-flag criteria to a student support team, multidisciplinary team, or other team in charge of planning Tier 2 and Tier 3 intervention (see Chapters 10 and 11 for more information).

Engaging and Supporting Staff in Attendance Efforts

To build a culture of attendance in your school, it is important for every staff member—including administrative, certified, and classified staff—to feel a sense of purpose and pride in implementing strategies to improve attendance. Although the attendance team will guide implementation efforts, your teaching staff will have the primary role in *selling* those efforts to your students and families. Therefore, staff buy-in is critical. In this chapter we provide strategies for engaging staff in attendance efforts, ensuring that they have a voice in the improvement process, and supporting them in implementing and maintaining your attendance initiative.

Get All Staff Members on Board

At the outset of the attendance initiative, allocate professional development time to work with staff so that they understand the negative effects of absenteeism on your school. Many staff members have probably heard or thought about the effects on academic outcomes; however, many have probably not thought about the range of other problems that may occur when students are frequently absent. Staff members may be reluctant to participate in planned lessons, motivational systems, or other activities if they simply view this work as a top-down initiative that will not greatly improve outcomes for their students or their own job satisfaction. Select from the following suggested activities or design your own to get staff members asking, "What can we all do to tackle this critical issue?"

Present Summaries of Research About Negative Effects of Absenteeism

Select information from Chapter 1 to share with staff, or search for studies relevant to your student population. Highlight information that is most relevant to your students' ages, demographics, and other conditions in your school such as cultural or linguistic diversity or socioeconomic levels of families.

Have Staff Brainstorm Negative Effects on the Student, Class, and Community/Society

The following activity often creates rich conversations about the seriousness of absenteeism issues and how they create rippling negative effects in all parts of a school and community. It can be a powerful way to help staff see that efforts to create a culture of attendance can have positive effects on everyone, leading to more productive and positive outcomes in schools and communities.

Figure 4.1 shows a sample handout that staff can use to brainstorm the ways that absenteeism may be affecting the school and society. Have staff members individually brainstorm negative effects for 5 to 10 minutes. Then have them join a partner or form small groups and share what they listed for each section. Finally, bring the whole staff back together and discuss some of the key points. It may also be helpful to pull in supporting research that might confirm or expand upon things that staff members are likely to observe, such as research indicating that absenteeism can slow down the learning of the whole class, not just the individual student (Musser, 2011).

Analyze and Present Data on Absenteeism in Your School

Prepare a presentation to help staff members understand the prevalence of absenteeism problems in your school and the relationship between attendance and students' academic outcomes. After informing staff about the negative effects of chronic absenteeism, present data on the percentage of students in your school in the Regular Attendance, At-Risk Attendance, Chronic Absence, and Severe Chronic Absence categories. Ensure that data are presented in an easy-to-understand format, such as a pie chart or bar graph instead of a long spreadsheet of days missed (see Figure 4.2 for

FIGURE 4.1 **Brainstorming Negative Effects with Staff**

What Are the Negative Effects of Absenteeism?		
For the Student	**For the Class and School**	**For Parents, Community, and Society**
Inside school:	The teacher:	Parents and families:
	Other students:	Local community:
Outside school:		
	The school:	Society:

FIGURE 4.2 **Pie Chart Showing Attendance Rates at a Middle School**

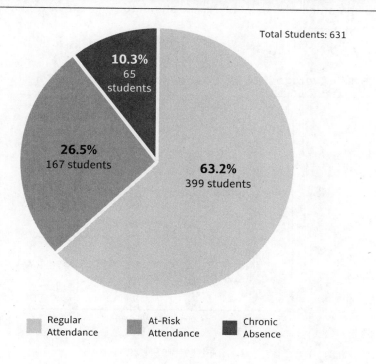

Total Students: 631

10.3%
65 students

26.5%
167 students

63.2%
399 students

Regular Attendance At-Risk Attendance Chronic Absence

an appropriate example). Note that the district that created the visual in Figure 4.2 collapsed the Severe Chronic and Chronic categories into one category to keep the data visualization as simple as possible. However, they analyze and discuss the number or percentage of students within the Chronic category who have missed 20 percent or more of the school year.

If this presentation occurs before the start of a new school year, present data from the previous year. In many schools, educators are shocked to learn the extent of absenteeism problems in their school. They may have been aware of a few students with extremely severe levels of absenteeism (e.g., 60 days, 90 days), but they may have thought this was an isolated issue involving just a few individuals. When the 10 percent criterion for Chronic Absence is used, educators see that a much greater percentage of students have levels of absenteeism that are cause for concern.

It may also be useful to analyze and discuss how these absenteeism rates relate to students' academic success. For example, graph the average GPA for students in each of the attendance categories: Regular Attendance, At-Risk Attendance, Chronic Absence, and Severe Chronic Absence. In most schools, such a graph will show a clear declining trend in GPAs as students move from regular to worse attendance categories (see Figure 4.3).

Here are some additional ways you might present absenteeism data for students in each attendance category:

- Percentage who meet or exceed standards on state or other standardized tests

FIGURE 4.3 **Average GPA by Attendance Category**

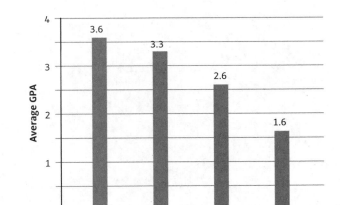

- Average DIBELS or Oral Reading Fluency scores
- Average number of behavioral referrals
- Percentage who graduated

For example, one district broke down its data according to graduation rates, looking at data across seven years. The district found that students with regular attendance (missing 5 percent or less of school) had a graduation rate of 91 percent. Students who were chronically absent (missing 10–20 percent of school days) had only a 68 percent graduation rate. Students who were severely chronically absent (missing 20–30 percent of school days) had a 26 percent graduation rate, and students who missed more than 30 percent of school days had less than a 5 percent likelihood of graduating. These data were powerful in helping staff understand the critical importance of everyone working together to improve attendance. Although the district and staff recognized that the data were correlational and they could not indicate with certainty that students' attendance was the cause of the differences in graduation rates, the data clearly indicated a relationship between attendance and graduation rates. This information was a powerful message when shared with students and families.

The data for subgroups of students can also be displayed to compare the prevalence of Chronic Absence and Severe Chronic Absence for students in a variety of subgroups (e.g., broken down by race or ethnicity, students with disabilities as compared to nonidentified peers, or students who receive free and reduced lunch as compared with students who do not). This data can be used to determine if absenteeism issues are affecting particular communities of students more than others, and to determine if additional efforts are needed to determine and address causes of absenteeism that are affecting these communities. Carefully consider how best to present this data to staff and the community. If less than 10 percent of your student population is in a particular subgroup, be particularly cautious in how this data is analyzed and presented since this percentage represents a relatively small number of students.

After building the rationale for the importance of this work, plan to present some initial universal strategies within the same staff development time so that staff leave with a sense of empowerment to tackle the issue. Select strategies from Chapters 5 through 8 that may be most likely to succeed, will be relatively easy for staff to implement, and may be fun or exciting for the school community. Consider presenting some success stories of schools that have effectively used the universal strategies in this book to significantly change their absenteeism rates. Figures 4.4 and 4.5 provide data from real schools, and additional examples of successful efforts appear throughout this book.

Figure 4.4 shows data from a group of pilot schools in Michigan that participated in a one-day training on the universal prevention procedures described in this book. As the figure shows, the year before the training the schools had approximately 20 to 45 percent of their students chronically absent between the start of school and winter break. After implementing universal procedures tailored to their schools, each school found that approximately 5 percent or fewer of their students were chronically absent from the start of school to winter break. They significantly reduced their absenteeism problems through universal prevention, creating space to intervene with the smaller number of students who had more resistant absenteeism issues.

Figure 4.5 presents data from Challenger High School, an alternative high school that serves the highest-risk students in a medium-sized district in Washington. Before the first year of intervention, the school ended the school year with an ADA of 77.2 percent. Starting in 2016–2017, the school implemented an Attendance Improvement Plan with the following components:

- Schoolwide expectation of regular attendance (missing no more than 5 percent of school days) was emphasized regularly by teachers in first period.
- Teachers charted first-period attendance, and each class received a reward when it reached an attendance goal.

FIGURE 4.4 **Percentage of Chronically Absent Students Before and After Universal Training**

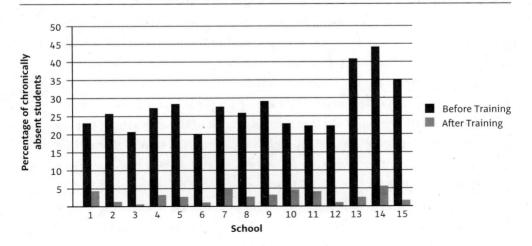

FIGURE 4.5 **Cumulative ADA Percentage at an Alternative High School Before and After Training**

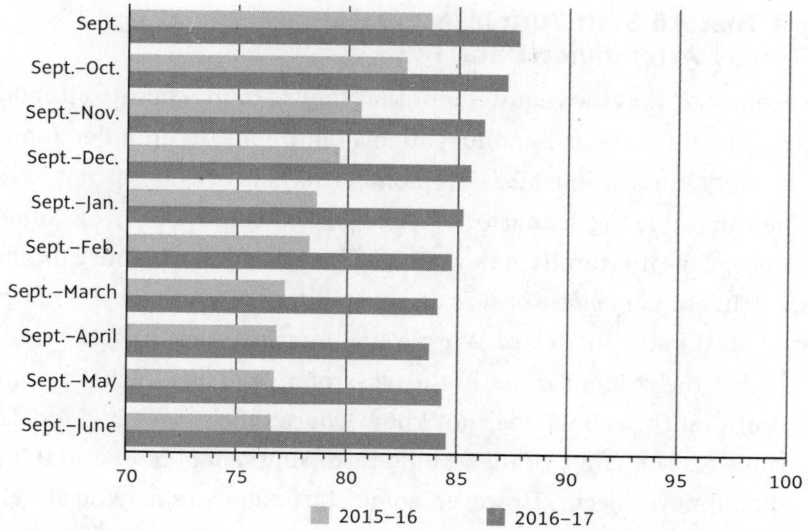

Source: Challenger High School Percentage of Average Daily Attendance. Adapted with permission from Challenger High School, Bethel, Washington.

- Students were recognized quarterly for regular and perfect attendance.
- Parents were educated about "How sick is too sick to come to school?"
- The attendance team met monthly to review data and identify students with attendance challenges.
- A support team met to provide support with students with chronic and severe chronic absence issues.

The principal was surprised at how easy it was to implement these simple preventive strategies and the immense difference they made. In one year, the school improved its ADA by 8.4 percentage points, which represented more than 4,300 days of increased attendance across the student body of 285 students! (See Appendix A for a detailed version of the Challenger High School Attendance Improvement Plan.)

Provide Supports for Staff to Implement Attendance Activities

The more the attendance team can support the staff in implementing attendance strategies, the more likely it is that the strategies will be effective. Methods of support range from helping teachers improve the efficiency of their attendance-taking routines to providing lesson plans that encourage student attendance and materials needed for implementation.

Ensure That All Staff Turn in Accurate and Timely Attendance Data

Inform staff that the requirement that they turn in accurate attendance data in a timely manner is nonnegotiable, and help them understand the serious safety implications if a staff member forgets or chooses not to do it. Imagine the following scenario: A parent unexpectedly calls or comes to school because of a family emergency. The attendance report indicates that the student is in class, or it is discovered that attendance has not been reported for the student's class. When a staff member goes to get the student, he finds that the student is not in the classroom, and he now has to inform the parent that the school does not know where the student is. Schools are responsible for the safety of their students during school hours, so this scenario should never occur. However, some staff members may need help to develop effective routines for taking and turning in their attendance. The following suggestions may be useful for staff members who struggle to take or turn in attendance.

Use assigned seats. Rather than roll call, which is the antithesis of an engaging start to a class (recall the attendance roll call in *Ferris Bueller's Day Off*: "Bueller . . . Bueller . . . Bueller . . ."), assigning seats allows a teacher to see at a glance which students are present. If the teacher wishes to allow students to choose their own seats, choose a day at the beginning of a month-long or two-week-long period for students to select their seats. Then create a seating chart and use the chart for the next several weeks.

Provide additional support for substitutes by taking a picture of the class, or by attaching student photos next to student names on the assigned-seating chart. This measure will allow substitute teachers to see that students are sitting in their assigned seats and not pretending to be someone else to be near a friend.

Use a warm-up or entry task. Within the first 5 or 10 minutes of class, have students complete a silent warm-up task at their seats to keep them instructionally engaged while the teacher takes and enters attendance.

Create an "attendance entry" or "attendance delivery" job. In some classrooms a teacher can create a job for a reliable student that involves using the assigned-seating chart to identify students who are absent. The student can provide these names to the teacher or in some cases enter the information into an attendance system without submitting it (the teacher should always double-check and then submit the information). Or the student might hand-deliver the attendance sheet to the office.

Provide regular reminders to staff to turn in attendance. Use students as teacher assistants (TAs) in the school office each period. When a classroom has not submitted attendance within the first 10 minutes of the day or period, have the TA walk to the class and give the teacher a reminder slip that says "Please turn in your attendance!"

Provide Support for Implementation of Attendance Efforts

To keep momentum going throughout each school year, the attendance team will need to provide ongoing support for staff members. Supply support through regular staff development or mini professional development opportunities and by providing materials and strategies in memos, e-mail messages, or other regular communication.

Be considerate of the dynamics of implementation in your school. For lack of a better term, we sometimes refer to these dynamics as "politics" as you consider how to negotiate things like staff unity relative to the initiative, staff preferences for autonomy and choice, and nature of communication among staff. There is a fine balance between minimizing the work teachers and other staff need to do by providing them with ready-made procedures and materials and giving them some choice as to what parts of the attendance initiative they implement, and how. If the team makes the decisions and creates the materials, teachers will have less work to do, but they may also have less buy-in to the system or strategy.

When possible, gather staff feedback, but be considerate of their time. The team should try to minimize the amount of work teachers and other staff will need to do outside staff meetings to implement strategies with their students. When in doubt, solicit staff feedback, as described in the next section.

Solicit Staff Feedback on Proposed Attendance Plans

Note: Material in this section is adapted with permission from Foundations: A Positive and Proactive Behavior Support System, *by R. Sprick, S. Isaacs, M. Booher, J. Sprick, and P. Rich.*

When an attendance team develops a plan that requires relatively little of staff, it may be appropriate simply to inform staff about the problem the plan seeks to address, specifics of the plan, and any role they will play in implementing it. However, if the plan will require significant effort or major changes for any staff members or if you anticipate resistance, solicit feedback and conduct activities to increase staff unity and buy-in before rolling out the plan.

Determine the amount of staff feedback and participation that will occur in developing and adopting a proposed attendance plan, keeping in mind the following considerations:

- A whole-staff approach is beneficial because it may increase buy-in and can be relatively quick to develop. However, it may require staff to put in additional work time to develop materials, and there is an increased possibility of poor implementation because staff may not have time to fully develop or learn about all parts of the plan.

- A team approach tends to be more carefully and systematically developed, but the pace of developing and adopting proposals can be slower than with a whole-staff approach.

Consider the politics of your staff when deciding which approach to use (both approaches are described in the following sections). Also consider factors such as these:

- Typical levels of staff resistance or support for trying new things and making changes
- Staff time available for voting on and giving feedback on proposals
- Staff workload for creating procedures and materials
- The amount of change required of staff members who are affected by the plan (the greater the change, the more staff feedback should be solicited)
- The desired pace of change

For example, if staff are highly resistant to change or are suffering from initiative fatigue, consider ways to get an easy win without requiring a lot of effort from staff members. In this case, a team approach is probably going to be most effective, and the team might focus on working with a few motivated teachers first so those individuals can provide testimonials that will get other teachers engaged. Then, once these staff members are on board, the attendance team can create procedures and materials needed for all staff to participate in implementing the plan. Alternatively, figure out a few high-leverage strategies that are easy to implement and do not require a lot of staff time and effort. For example, have the attendance team create memos that can be sent home to indicate the importance of attendance and create several lesson plans that staff can deliver to students. Then, once staff members have bought in, the team can determine a more comprehensive implementation plan. If staff prefer to be more engaged in the development process and would like to move more quickly with implementation, a whole-staff approach is likely to be preferable.

Develop a Plan Using Option 1: The Whole-Staff Approach

In a whole-staff approach, the entire staff is included, and staff members may be divided into groups to tackle different issues. For example, groups might create a plan and materials for one of the following strategies, which are described in detail in later chapters, as indicated:

- **Kickoff attendance assembly** (Chapter 5). This group plans a school-wide assembly to kick off the attendance initiative. Members identify staff members or guests who will speak about the importance of attendance and introduce schoolwide motivational systems and other aspects of the plan. The group decides when the assembly will occur, how to invite parents and community members, and other logistical matters.

- **Ongoing communication methods to connect with families** (Chapter 7). This group determines ways to communicate about attendance efforts and data with families, such as robocalls, memos, newsletter or social media updates. Members plan topics and materials for tips sheets (e.g., sleep, health, and hygiene tips) and determine how best to update families about the school's data and goals as well as individual student attendance.

- **Posters and flyers in the community** (Chapter 7). This group is responsible for designing, creating, and putting up posters and flyers advertising the attendance initiative in prominent locations in the community. Members connect with local businesses, medical providers, and other relevant locations to inform them about the school's goals and ask if they can place informational materials in highly visible locations.

- **Classroom motivational systems** (Chapter 5). This group creates classroom motivational systems for each grade level or the whole school. Members design simple daily attendance charts for each classroom and a structured reinforcement system that can be used to provide group motivation to attend school.

- **Classroom lessons** (Chapter 6). This group creates a small library of attendance lessons that will be delivered by each classroom teacher. Each short lesson (5 to 15 minutes) is designed to increase student awareness of the importance of attendance or to teach students strategies for overcoming attendance obstacles such as lack of sleep, illness, or transportation to school.

When tackling a difficult or complex issue, a whole-staff approach might also involve breaking the staff into small groups and having each group come up with ideas. For example, if the school identifies that absences for school- and club-related activities are causing significant problems, have small groups brainstorm ideas to address this issue. Have the groups present their ideas to the whole staff, and have staff indicate which strategies seem most promising and which they are concerned about and why. The attendance team can then take this information and develop a plan for the staff.

An elementary school in Florida initially used the whole-school approach in various areas—playground, arrival, dismissal, halls, restrooms, and cafeteria—with every staff member being part of a task force for an area. The effort proved so successful in improving the climate of the school and the behavior of students that it also resulted in staff receiving a greater sense of empowerment and collegiality. Two years later, when their data indicated that attendance would be their big priority for the following year, they created five task-force groups related to attendance: messaging to parents of preK to 1st grade students, messaging to parents of students in grades 2 through 6, messaging to students, providing community outreach, and developing a schoolwide reward system based on attendance. Because of previous success, the staff was excited to take on this challenge.

Develop a Plan Using Option 2:
The Attendance Team Approach

In an attendance team approach, the team does the preliminary work to develop a plan for staff. If the team develops a proposal to address a specific priority, invite additional personnel who are relevant to planning meetings. For example, if morning arrival is problematic and contributes to attendance problems, invite a representative of bus drivers and any classified or certified staff who supervise morning arrival so they can provide input on problems and possible solutions. If the team is working on ways to increase parent participation and buy-in with the attendance initiative, invite parent representatives to work with the team on a plan.

As the proposal is being developed, solicit staff feedback yet be considerate of their time. Here are some ways to get guidance without taking too much staff time:

- Hold a 10-minute brainstorming session during a faculty meeting (no evaluating of ideas or extension of the time allowed). If the discussion becomes contentious or significant problems or concerns are identified, plan to revisit the discussion at a later staff meeting, or invite staff with concerns to join the next attendance team meeting.
- Write the proposal, issue, or question on a poster in the staff room. Ask staff to respond in writing.
- Write options for solving an issue on a poster in the staff room. Have staff members vote for their preferred option by writing their initials next to the suggestions they think will be most successful.

A middle school in California offers an example of the successful use of the team approach. The school identified that a significant percentage of the student population was chronically absent. During the same year, the district had adopted a new teacher observation and evaluation system, along with sequenced professional development to assist all teachers in mastering the skills that the system would evaluate. Because of the intensive demands this new evaluation system put on all teachers, it was decided that the bulk of the work on absenteeism would be done by the school's active and effective PBIS team. The team, including several highly respected teachers, led the charge of developing universal procedures to improve attendance. Because the staff was professional and largely united, they implemented lessons for students and sent messages to parents. The staff appreciated that the PBIS team had done the bulk of the work. Within two years, the rate of chronic absence was greatly reduced.

Adopt a Plan

Once the proposal is developed, present it to the whole staff during a five-minute presentation at a staff meeting. At least two days before the meeting, share the plan by e-mail or put copies of it into mailboxes. At the meeting, provide no more than 10 minutes for staff members to discuss the proposal and ask questions, then use a system for reaching consensus on the adoption or rejection of the proposal.

At the meeting, consider using the Five Levels of Satisfaction System, in which staff members publicly show their support or lack of support for a proposal by rating it on a five-point scale, using their fingers:

> 5 fingers = I support the proposal wholeheartedly and am willing to help with it.
> 4 fingers = I support the proposal wholeheartedly.
> 3 fingers = The proposal is fine. I neither like nor dislike it.
> 2 fingers = I am uncomfortable with the proposal but will go along if more than 90 percent of the staff accepts it. I will not be a passive or active obstructionist.
> 1 finger = I cannot live with the proposal and am willing to help the team develop an alternative.

It is important to note that if even one person puts up one finger, the proposal is rejected, but anyone doing so must agree to work to help find an alternative to the proposal. In our experience, one-finger votes are rare because of the requirement that the person do follow-up work to revise the proposal. If this occurs, it is often because of legitimate concerns that were overlooked in making the proposal, and the additional work done to revise the proposal results in a stronger plan with greater likelihood of success.

If the staff members vote to adopt the proposal, the team moves forward with steps for implementation. If the proposal is rejected, the team (and any staff members who voted 1) work to develop an alternative proposal based on staff feedback. They then present the alternative proposal to staff for another vote. After two attempts to revise (a total of three voting cycles), the issue should go to the principal, who will make the final decision. This procedure prevents the staff from being endlessly stuck on one issue. Note that divisive issues are best resolved by a principal who says, "This is what we are going to do and here's why."

Some years ago, Randy had the opportunity to work with a large middle school on implementing *Foundations*, Safe & Civil Schools' approach to schoolwide behavior support. An established norm was that any work done by the *Foundations* group or a task force would include limited debate (a maximum of 10 minutes) during staff meetings. A task force had been working on a proposal to identify what types of behavior could warrant removing a student from class for disciplinary reasons. The task force had given their proposal in writing to staff two days earlier and asked that they review it in preparation for the 10-minute discussion. Randy was facilitating the discussion during the staff meeting and after 8 minutes thought the group had reached consensus, so he called for a five-finger vote. When one person held up one finger, some other staff members groaned in frustration. Randy said, "Please wait. A vote of 1 represents a strongly held position and a willingness to be part of the solution. Let's respect that." He then said to the objector, "We have one minute left. Would you like to summarize your concerns to the group now, or just be part of the next task force meeting?" The staff member then summarized an issue that no one else had considered, and some of the people who had groaned acknowledged that they hadn't thought about that particular concern. Two weeks later at the next staff meeting, the task force, along with the person who had voted 1, presented their revised proposal and every staff member voted 4 or 5. The lesson here is that sometimes in the rush to complete business quickly, it's easy to overlook critical factors. The five-finger vote can ensure that critical and thoughtful dissent is heard and problems can be addressed.

Implement a Plan

Consider what materials, training (for staff, students, and families), and support are needed when implementing new policies or procedures. Also plan to review and evaluate the success or failure of any changes that were implemented by staff after four to six weeks of implementation—ensure that staff members know that the plan and the timeline will be reviewed. This step is critical and allows you to assure skeptical or resistant staff members that the team will evaluate the plan to see if it is having a positive, neutral, or negative impact. The goal is to ask all staff to implement the plan with fidelity to ensure that the procedures do not fail because of passive or active resistance.

If data indicate that procedures are having a positive effect, share the good news with staff, students, and families. If procedures are having a negative or neutral impact, determine whether staff implementation is a problem. If so, work to motivate and better prepare the staff through additional training, creative reminders (e.g., a staff raffle based on staff participation with a student motivational system), or administrative emphasis. If implementation is not the problem, reconvene the attendance team to develop a revised or new proposal for staff consideration.

✓ **Sunrise Middle School Scenario** Staff members at Sunrise were initially skeptical that they could make a significant difference with attendance. They also felt that this issue should not take precedence over other academic and behavioral initiatives, so there was some resistance to implementing an intensive attendance plan. However, when the attendance team presented the school's data indicating that 35 percent of Sunrise students were in the At-Risk Attendance or Chronic Absence categories, the teachers agreed that they would implement simple strategies in their classes as long as these strategies did not require a lot of time or effort. The attendance team worked over the summer to prepare a memo that would be sent home before the start of school indicating the school's new goal of every student having regular attendance. They also prepared lessons that teachers would present in the first two weeks of school and articles about the attendance initiative for the first several issues of the school newsletter. Finally, the team created a simple bar graph for classroom teachers showing the attendance for each class throughout the day, and a system for rewarding a class when it had 10 days of perfect attendance.

Initially, some staff members expressed frustration at having to use the classroom graph and motivational system; however, the team emphasized that teachers would need to use the graphs for only four weeks. At that time, the team would consult with the staff to determine if the systems were too onerous and examine the data to see if attendance was improving. They asked all teachers to implement the plan with fidelity for four weeks so that they could collectively assess whether the plan was appropriate and making a difference. After the first month of school, even the teachers who had been the most resistant indicated that the systems were not too time consuming and seemed to be making a significant difference in attendance. Many teachers shared other positive effects, like students cheering for one another when peers walked in the door and the class met the day's goal, and some students asking if they could call to check on absent peers and tell them they were missed when they were absent. The staff members voted to formally adopt the classroom motivational systems as long as the data continued to show positive effects.

■ ■ ■ ■ ■

In this chapter we have provided strategies for engaging and supporting staff members in your school's attendance efforts. Staff—particularly teachers—are the people who have the most influence on students and families, so it is essential to ensure that they are engaged, active, and empowered participants in the effort to build a schoolwide culture of attendance. Whereas the first four chapters of this book have focused on laying the groundwork for effective team functioning and school processes to ensure staff buy-in, the remaining chapters will focus on strategies that you can use at the schoolwide and individual levels to improve attendance. The next chapter, which provides a range of strategies for kicking off and then sustaining your attendance campaign, is followed by chapters that discuss ways to teach students and families about the importance of regular attendance and how to achieve it.

■ ■ ■ ■ ■

Summary of Tasks for Engaging and Supporting Staff

Use the following outline as a quick reminder of the tasks involved in engaging and supporting staff in your attendance efforts.

Conduct initial activities to get all staff members on board.

- Identify strategies that you will use to get initial buy-in from all staff members.
- Indicate when you plan to use these strategies and who will prepare necessary procedures and materials.

Provide supports for staff to implement attendance activities.

- Identify ways that staff may require support in order to implement and maintain your attendance initiative and who will be responsible for providing support.
- List dates in each quarter or term when you will evaluate whether staff members are receiving necessary supports to make attendance plans successful.

Solicit staff feedback on proposed attendance plans.

- As the team identifies priorities and makes decisions, solicit staff feedback as necessary. List at least two dates during the year when the team will evaluate whether approaches for soliciting feedback are effective.

5

Creating and Sustaining
an Attendance Campaign

One definition of *campaign* in the Merriam-Webster Dictionary is "a connected series of operations designed to bring about a particular result." The
work you do to create a culture of attendance in your school can be viewed as
an ongoing campaign with connected operations, including initial efforts to
build enthusiasm and momentum and continued efforts to sustain the active
engagement of all stakeholders in the goal of improving attendance. In this
chapter we describe strategies for kicking off an attendance initiative and
methods for keeping up the momentum across years through motivational
systems and ongoing communication.

Kick Off the Attendance Campaign

After conducting activities to get all staff members on board, consider how
best to launch the attendance campaign with students, families, and community members. Work to generate excitement and interest. We suggest a two-
stage process. First, to create enthusiasm, develop a title or slogan. Then, to
announce the title or slogan, launch an official campaign, which can include
strategies such as classroom kickoffs, publicity at back-to-school or parent
nights, and other strategies described in this chapter.

All kickoff strategies should share the rationale for why attendance is
essential for success in school and in life and present information on the
critical goal of regular attendance (missing 5 percent or fewer school days)

and avoiding chronic absence (missing 10 percent or more school days). The more times and ways in which you share information about the attendance campaign, the more likely you are to create the momentum needed to change the culture of attendance in your school. The next sections provide examples of ways to publicize the attendance campaign.

Create a Title or Slogan

Work as a team or whole staff to generate ideas for a title or slogan for the attendance campaign. This phrase should speak to the importance of attendance and the cultural value that the school places on students being in school, learning, every day. It should be used like a mantra. Embed it into all subsequent discussions and materials used for the attendance campaign (e.g., posters, lessons, memos to families). When possible, incorporate your school mascot, concepts from your mission or vision statement, or the name of the school. Here are some examples of slogans:

- Roosevelt Eagles soar to success with regular attendance.
- We are dependable, persistent, and attend each day.
- The Lions: Our pride comes to school, ready to learn every day.

To generate enthusiasm for the campaign, you might consider introducing the basic concepts of the attendance initiative in an assembly or other kickoff method and announcing a competition for students to generate a representative title or slogan. After compiling the suggestions, students can vote for the winning campaign title or slogan, which will appear on all future materials and attendance efforts. This approach may increase student enthusiasm and buy-in, but it will require that the school delay printing posters and other publicity materials for the attendance initiative; so carefully consider how much this activity may interest and benefit your students and families. If this approach is appealing, you will need to take steps before the kickoff assembly to determine how the slogan competition will be conducted—from encouraging brainstorming that gets staff, students, and families involved to the final selection.

Hold an Attendance Assembly

Regardless of the method you choose to create a slogan, consider launching your campaign with an assembly specifically focused on teaching students about the importance of attendance. Provide information on the topic but remember to keep the focus on generating enthusiasm. This assembly should feel like a pep rally. Consider the following ideas for generating excitement:

- Invite a local public figure (e.g., sports star, television personality) or motivational speaker who can convey the importance of students being in school every day. Work with the speaker to generate specific talking points related to the attendance campaign.
- Have a school team (e.g., cheerleaders, dance team, drama team) perform, or invite a local performance team from the community. If the performance does not have a direct link to attendance, create a banner or other materials that can be used throughout the performance to emphasize the attendance message.
- Create an attendance chant or use the school's selected attendance slogan and have different parts of the audience compete to give the most convincing cheer.
- Introduce any schoolwide motivational systems and possible rewards that will be used in the subsequent term or semester. (See page 82 for examples of schoolwide motivational systems and rewards.)
- Create school T-shirts with the attendance slogan or goal printed on them and randomly toss them into the audience throughout the assembly.

Ensure that any individuals who are invited to address the students are engaging speakers who can speak convincingly about the importance of this initiative and select staff members who are well liked and respected by students to be part of the presentation. Members of the school administration should be visible and engaged throughout the assembly to show their commitment to these efforts.

Use Classroom Kickoffs

After an attendance assembly, or when a schoolwide assembly is not possible, emphasize the key points of the attendance initiative in each classroom. Administrators, counseling or other interventionist staff, or members of the attendance team might rotate to classes throughout the day and give a short presentation on the attendance initiative. The attendance team could also prepare a presentation (e.g., a slide show or a scripted lesson) that each teacher delivers to students.

Publicize at Back-to-School or Parent Nights

To launch the initiative with parents, create a presentation focused on attendance and present the information whenever you anticipate having a large number of parents in the school. Emphasize relevant research findings and the negative effects of absenteeism (see Chapter 1 for possible talking points). It may also be useful to conduct the brainstorming activity from Chapter 4 (see page 56) and have parents discuss the negative effects of absenteeism on the student, the class, and the larger community/society. Provide relevant materials and strategies that can help parents work as partners with the school to improve their children's attendance (see strategies on the following pages and in Chapter 7).

Send an Initial Letter Home

Send home an initial letter or pass one out at the parent presentation. The letter should inform parents about the attendance initiative, indicate why it is important for students to regularly attend school, and provide information about measures the school will take to partner with families to problem-solve when it is difficult to get a student to school regularly. The tone of this letter should be welcoming and supportive. Avoid placing emphasis on punitive measures such as fines or truancy court. See Figure 5.1 for an example. Note that the letter refers to an attendance chart, which is described in the next paragraph.

Provide an Attendance Chart

Send home a chart that the student and family can use to monitor absences across the year. Inform the students and families that any time the student is absent, they should fill in one of the spaces on the chart. Design the chart to reflect the number of absences that would place the student in the Regular Attendance category at the end of the year (e.g., include nine spaces if the school has 180 days of school).

If possible, color-code the absences: absences 1 through 9 should be green, and absences 10 and up should be yellow or red to indicate increasing risk. Be sure to note that the student is at increased risk for academic difficulties and other struggles at school with each subsequent absence beyond the spaces provided on the chart. Print the chart on card stock or laminate it.

The goal of this chart is to provide a tool for busy students and families to maintain a better sense of how many absences the student accumulates

FIGURE 5.1 **Initial Attendance Letter**

DEDICATED TO ACADEMIC EXCELLENCE

Loganville Middle School
4321 Any Street
Townsville, State 54321

Dear families,

We are looking forward to a great year, with students in classes and ready to learn every day.

We have learned that students who miss even a few days of school each month are at far greater risk of academic failure and dropping out than students who attend regularly. We have set a goal that every student in our school attend regularly (has nine or fewer absences in a year).

Because attendance is so important, please send your child to school every day unless he or she has a contagious illness or is running a fever.

We have included a chart with this letter that will help you keep track of your student's absences. If your child is at risk of missing too much school, please feel free to contact Joan Ndogo at 555-1234 for assistance. We will also monitor each student's attendance across the year so we can work with families when the number of absences puts a student at risk. We will be happy to work with you to help your student attend regularly and have greater opportunities for success.

Sincerely,

Aaron Chan, Principal

Source: From *Foundations Module C, Conscious Construction of an Inviting School Climate*, by R. Sprick, J. Sprick, and P. Rich, 2014, Eugene, OR: Pacific Northwest Publishing. Copyright © 2014 by Pacific Northwest Publishing. Used with permission.

FIGURE 5.2 **Generic Attendance Chart**

Date	Date	Date	Date	Date	Date	Date	Date	Date	Absence 10+
Absence 1 Reason:	Absence 2 Reason:	Absence 3 Reason:	Absence 4 Reason:	Absence 5 Reason:	Absence 6 Reason:	Absence 7 Reason:	Absence 8 Reason:	Absence 9 Reason:	Your student is at increasing risk for academic difficulties and school failure with each absence beyond this point.

throughout the year. See Figures 5.2, 5.3, and 5.4 for sample attendance charts.

First Creek Middle School in Washington creates refrigerator magnets (Figure 5.3) for each student. At open house night, school counselors speak to students and families about the importance of attendance and hand out the magnets. First Creek also includes an attendance tracker in student planners (Figure 5.4). When a student returns from an absence, the student's advisory

FIGURE 5.3 **Sample Attendance Magnet**

First Creek Middle School Attendance Matters!

A whole year has 365 days.
A school year has only 181 days.
That leaves 185 days to spend on family time, visits, holidays,
shopping, household jobs, and other appointments.

0–9 Days Absent 100%–95% Attendance	10–17 Days Absent 94%–90% Attendance	18+ Days Absent 89% Attendance or Less
Very Good Best chance of success. Gets your child off to a solid start.	**Worrying** Less chance for school success. Makes it harder for your child to make progress.	**Serious Concern** Your child will find it very difficult to make progress. May result in court action and likely route to dropping out.

Track your child's absences

1st	2nd	3rd	4th	5th	6th	7th	8th	9th	DANGER!
									Your child is at risk of school failure.

FIGURE 5.4 Sample Attendance Chart for Student Planners

Good Attendance for Success
Every Minute in School Counts

Attendance matters to your school success! Good attendance is missing not more than 1 day of school a month, whether excused or unexcused. Chronically absent is when you miss 18 school days a year or 2 days a month.

Students with good attendance:

- **Read better.**
- **Have higher GPAs.**
- **Will be on track for high school graduation.**

Attendance Tracker

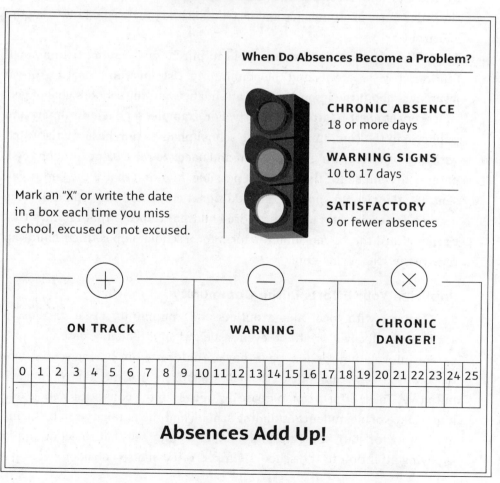

When Do Absences Become a Problem?

CHRONIC ABSENCE
18 or more days

WARNING SIGNS
10 to 17 days

SATISFACTORY
9 or fewer absences

Mark an "X" or write the date in a box each time you miss school, excused or not excused.

⊕										⊖								⊗						
ON TRACK										WARNING								CHRONIC DANGER!						
0	1	2	3	4	5	6	7	8	9	10	11	12	13	14	15	16	17	18	19	20	21	22	23	24	25

Absences Add Up!

teacher directs the student to open the planner and mark the absence on the tracker. This procedure can facilitate awareness and important conversations between the staff member and the student when a student is absent often.

Provide a Kickoff Item for Each Student

Purchase alarm clocks, specially designed attendance T-shirts, or another item that represents your initiative. Search for items that can be purchased in bulk for a relatively low price—$1 to $5 per student, for example—and determine the amount of money needed to provide the item to each enrolled student. The item should be used to generate enthusiasm and pride in the initiative. For example, consider alarm clock wristwatches with the school name or logo printed on the wristband, or alarm clock key chains that can be attached to students' backpacks. When the alarm clocks are passed out to students at an assembly or in classes, provide a corresponding lesson on the importance of attendance and instruction and practice on how to set the alarm clock.

If the school or district is unable to purchase the item, hold a small fundraiser with parents and the community. Use this fundraiser to spread awareness about the importance of attendance and the school's goal of getting every student to attend regularly. For example, send a letter home and publicize in the community that the school plans to purchase a wristwatch with an alarm clock for every student and needs to raise $2 per student. Ask parents to send $2 for their child, if possible. Mention that if the family can send $4, they would sponsor one additional child, and $10 would provide a watch for their child and four more children. Indicate that families that cannot afford the $2 can submit a form for a scholarship so their child can receive the schoolwide item.

Publicize Your Efforts in the Community

Connect with local media outlets and community organizations to see if they will cover or attend events such as an attendance assembly or a parent information session, or if they are interested in having school representatives come and speak to their organization about the attendance initiative. These efforts can increase awareness in the community about the importance of all students attending school, and the publicity can be highly motivating for staff, students, and families as they see that the community is paying attention to the school's efforts. You can also consider sending a school representative or group (e.g., staff, student, parent representatives) to prominent meetings in the community or provide informational pamphlets or posters for local businesses and community centers. Consider publicizing using the following media and opportunities:

- Television stations
- Radio stations
- School board
- City council
- City business associations
- After-school programs and community centers

Chapter 7 provides additional information about how to enhance community involvement.

Use Schoolwide and Classroom Motivational Systems

Once you have launched the attendance campaign, the work of maintaining momentum begins. It is the team's job to keep a focus on attendance and do the creative work to make the initiative compelling and fun. The effort is similar to an ad campaign for a new product (e.g., launching and sustaining a new brand of toothpaste) or movement (e.g., Smokey Bear and "Only you can prevent forest fires"). Schoolwide and classroom motivational systems are simple and efficient ways to maintain a focus on the attendance initiative. They have numerous benefits, including the following:

- Daily tracking and discussion of attendance in a motivational system sends a regular message that attendance is important.
- Staff and student awareness of attendance trends is heightened through the routine of the system.
- Students take pride in how their attendance contributes to the class or school progress in the system.
- Students are encouraged to work together, which can be beneficial for creating a sense of community and reaching collective goals.
- Class and staff preparation time is minimally affected.
- Easily implemented adaptations can maintain interest and provide a needed boost during times when absenteeism is most problematic.

It may be beneficial to select one or more systems that are carried throughout the entire year (e.g., charts showing percentages for daily schoolwide attendance and classroom attendance) and bring in other systems during particularly problematic times of year or when enthusiasm for the attendance initiative is waning. These additional systems could include, for example, month-by-month goals, raffles, or competitions between rival schools or classes within a grade level.

The following sections provide examples of schoolwide and classroom motivational systems for students, as well as systems that can be designed to increase teacher and staff participation and enthusiasm for attendance efforts. See Appendix B for schoolwide, classroom, and individual student reinforcers that can be part of any of these systems.

Schoolwide Motivational Systems

Schoolwide motivational systems can take many forms, and the following are a few examples of possible schoolwide motivational systems. Select one or more of the following (or design your own motivational systems) depending on the magnitude of attendance problems in your school.

Daily schoolwide attendance percentage. Publicly post the school's daily attendance rate. Create a large chart that shows the percentage of students who are in school each day and display it in the window of the front office or another high-visibility, high-traffic location (see the example in Figure 5.5). Announce the percentage of students who attended the previous day during the morning announcements, or have teachers announce the percentage in class. Each classroom teacher might also have a smaller version of the display in the classroom, and when the announcement is read, the teacher or a student could mark the percentage on the graph.

To increase the efficacy of this system, set a schoolwide goal and create an incentive structure that reinforces students when they reach their collective goal. Set a goal that is approximately two percentage points above the Average Daily Attendance (ADA) rate from the previous year or term. For example, if the previous year's ADA was 93 percent, draw a goal line on the chart at 95 percent. Determine possible schoolwide reinforcers that could be earned when the school reaches its goal (e.g., ice cream party, field day, hat day). Determine how many times the students must meet or exceed the goal to earn a schoolwide reward. A general principle is to provide the reinforcement relatively quickly at first (e.g., the reward is earned when the goal is met three times) and then gradually increase the number of days

FIGURE 5.5 **Graph of Daily Schoolwide Attendance**

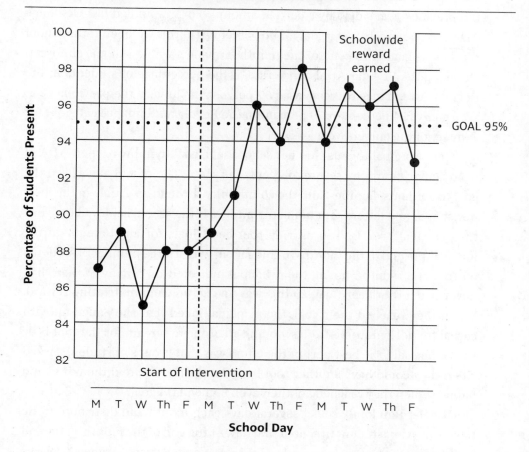

or the percentage that must be earned. Consider a reinforcement schedule such as this:

- Three days meeting the goal of 95 percent
- Five days meeting the goal of 95 percent
- Eight days meeting the goal of 95 percent (then increase by two points)
- Three days meeting the goal of 97 percent
- Five days meeting the goal of 97 percent
- Eight days meeting the goal of 97 percent

Month-by-month goals. Gather month-by-month data from the previous year. Consider using the ADA data each month or the percentage of students in the Regular Attendance category (missing no more than 5 percent of school days each month). Each month, set a schoolwide goal to improve over the previous year's data by a certain amount. For example, if last October's ADA was 94 percent, set a goal for 96 percent ADA this October. If the school reaches its goal at the end of the month, provide a whole-school reinforcer. Or, using the Regular Attendance rate, if the percentage of students in the Regular Attendance category was 69 percent in January the previous year, set a goal of 74 percent or 79 percent in the Regular Attendance category for January of the current year.

One principal told us that her school set a goal to improve their ADA in a particular month by several percentage points. The school advertised the goal to students, families, and the community through an article in the local newspaper and letters sent home to families. If the school achieved the goal, the principal promised to provide root beer floats for all students during lunch at the end of the month. In this school with a large number of students on free and reduced lunch, the principal indicated that many of them had never had a root beer float, so this was an exciting and motivating reward. When they reached their goal, the principal joked that she ended up with carpal tunnel syndrome from scooping all of the ice cream for the root beer floats! She said the best part of the effort was that groups of students asked when they could have another root beer float party. She told them it would happen when they reached another, even higher ADA goal.

Raffle. Randomly select several days each month and distribute raffle tickets to every student in school that day. At the end of the month, gather all raffle tickets for entry into a schoolwide drawing. Provide a range of prizes for individual students, including many small prizes, a moderate number of medium-value prizes, and a few grand prizes. During problematic times of the year (e.g., the week before and after a major break), increase the frequency of raffle ticket distribution and prize delivery so that students in school during these times have a greater chance of winning the prizes.

Principal's 200 Club. *Note: This strategy is adapted with permission from* The Tough Kid Principal's Briefcase *(Jenson et al., 2013).*

Create a large laminated poster that shows 200 cells numbered from 1 to 200 (e.g., 20 rows of 10 columns). Place this visual in a high-visibility, high-traffic area of the school (e.g., in the main hallway or window of the front office). Create 200 chips (e.g., poker chips or similar sized rounds of card stock) and label them 1 to 200. Place the chips in an opaque bucket, bag, or other container.

Select approximately 10 reinforcers or prizes that would be of value for a small group of individual students (e.g., pizza party, lunch with the principal, VIP parking in front of the school). Write the name of each reinforcer on an index card, fold the card, and place it in a Mystery Motivator prize container. On the first day of implementing the motivational system, select one card and seal it in a "secrecy envelope." Draw a question mark on the envelope and attach it to the poster.

Each day, randomly select 10 student names from the student body. Look at the attendance record and call any of the 10 students who have been regularly present since the start of school or term and ask them to sign the Celebrity Attendance Book. This is a dedicated book to record the names of students recognized in the Principal's 200 Club system. If possible, use or create a book that looks official and professional, not a plain spiral-bound notebook or binder. Call each student's parents and congratulate them and the student for being in school and helping to create a culture of attendance in the school. If parents are not home, mail a postcard or letter of congratulations.

Before the celebrity students return to class, have each one draw a numbered chip from the container. Write the student's name in erasable marker on the corresponding number on the poster. Do not return the numbered chip to the container. However, ensure that the students' names go back onto the list of names in the student body so that they have a chance at winning a prize again if they continue to be in attendance.

Whenever a row or column is full, the students whose names appear in that row or column receive the Mystery Motivator. Announce their names during the morning announcements and call them down to the office to receive the prize or information about when the prize will be delivered. Erase all names from the poster and begin again.

Friendly school competitions. Create friendly competitions within the school or in partnership with other schools nearby. Ensure that corresponding lessons are taught to students on encouraging peers to attend (as opposed to bullying or threatening), how to be a good winner and a good loser, and ways to work together toward improvements. Friendly competitions can be developed around targets such as these:

- The grade with the most improved ADA or regular attendance rate over the previous month

- The grade or class with the highest ADA or regular attendance rate each month or term
- The class with the highest ADA each week
- The school with the most improved ADA from the previous year or month

Two middle schools in Fresno, California, challenged each other to an attendance competition. Gaston Middle School and Sequoia Middle School competed to see which school could have the most improved ADA for one month in the fall. The staff of the school with less improvement had to wear the other school's T-shirts for a day. Each school's ADA improved by more than two percentage points (Gaston's ADA went from 91.57 percent to 93.71 percent, and Sequoia's went from 91.02 percent to 93.47 percent), representing more than 300 days of instruction gained at each school in one month. The schools have continued to push for attendance improvements. They set a year-long goal of 95 percent ADA or better and implemented strategies such as a period-by-period schoolwide competition in which classes with 100 percent attendance and zero tardies for a day color a letter on a chart; when all the letters are filled in, the class gets healthy snacks.

Celebrations of attendance. Hold a monthly or term/semester celebration of attendance with a school assembly or community event. Use these opportunities to reteach and show enthusiasm for the school's efforts to build a culture of attendance.

Many schools already hold these kinds of celebrations, but the focus is on acknowledging students who have perfect attendance. Unfortunately, perfect attendance is not realistic for many students and not recommended in certain circumstances. Students often face significant barriers that are out of their control (e.g., parents who can't or won't get students to school regularly, or students with chronic illness). These awards can have a punitive effect for those who may want to get to school each day but are unable to despite their best efforts and the support of the school. Furthermore, awards for perfect attendance may push some students to come to school when they have a contagious illness. If they come simply to preserve their attendance records, they may spread the illness and cause other students to be absent.

Rather than awards for perfect attendance, consider recognizing students in the Regular Attendance category and those with improved attendance. For example, if a student moves from the Chronic Absence category in one month to At-Risk or Regular Attendance the following month, provide an "Improved Attendance" award.

Whole-school classroom attendance. In this system, each class works toward having 10 days at or above a class goal (e.g., 96 percent attendance). If this system is set up at the beginning of the year, you may decide to use a standard goal across all classes (e.g., each classroom aims for 97 percent attendance). However, if this is a midyear effort, have each class set its own goal. Each teacher should look at class attendance data for two or three weeks before rollout of the system and use those data to set the goal. For example, one teacher might find that on the best day, 2 students out of 30 were absent, but on most days, 3 to 6 were absent. That teacher might set a goal so that if only 2 students are absent (93 percent attendance), the class reaches the goal. In a class that had one day with no one absent and most days with only 1 or 2 students absent, the teacher might set the goal at 100 percent.

For each classroom, create a visual display that has 10 spaces or pieces that need to be filled in or added to the display. Each day that a class meets the goal, they add a piece to their display. When the class fills the display by meeting the goal, they earn group incentives and schoolwide recognition.

McLean Elementary School in Wichita, Kansas, used a Mr. Potato Head toy as the classroom-based visual system in their "No Tardy Tators" initiative, which was designed to increase the number of students present during the first hour of the school day. Each class selected 10 pieces for their Mr. Potato Head toy figure. Whenever a class met its attendance goal for the day, they added a piece to the body. When all pieces were added to the figure, the class earned a group reward, such as a certificate of attendance delivered to the class by the principal. The certificate is displayed outside the classroom door to create friendly competition among classes and to display the school's pride and emphasis on a culture of attendance. One class chose to have Crazy Sock Day. All students wore crazy socks to school, and their teacher took a picture of their feet while they were lying in a circle.

In the first quarter of the year before the No Tardy Tators initiative, McLean Elementary had 224 tardies at the beginning of the day. The following year, there were 118 tardies in the first quarter. The second quarter saw a similar significant reduction in tardies—from 350 the year before to 179 with No Tardy Tators in place. Although the motivational system did not completely eliminate the start-of-day tardy problem, it significantly reduced it, with very little time, cost, or effort from staff.

Furthermore, staff and students shared numerous testimonials of how the initiative made a major difference for individual students. Principal Mendie Vicin shared this example:

> At the beginning of the year, we had a family that was tardy the first three days of school. On the third day, the mother called me to ask about "this Potato Head thing" her daughters were telling her about. I explained our No Tardy Tators program and how we are all working together to earn Mr. Potato Head [toy decoration] pieces. This family has not had a single tardy since that day—93 days so far!

With similar enthusiasm, a student said this:

> I love our Mr. Potato Head [toy]! We get to take turns putting the pieces on him, and when we get 10 we get a certificate and potato head to put on the wall. I don't want to be late, so sometimes I tell my mom, "Hurry up and drive fast because I don't want to be late!"

Another example of a successful attendance initiative comes from Barnes Elementary School in Kelso, Washington, whose mascot is a bear. The school created templates of bears and items of clothing for each class. For each day a class met its goal, the students chose and added a piece of clothing to the bear. See Appendix A for a description of the Barnes attendance initiative.

At the secondary level, teachers at Challenger High School in Spanaway, Washington, charted first-period attendance on a classroom graph (see page 91 for an explanation of how to create a daily attendance graph). Because the previous year's ADA was 75 percent, the classrooms set a goal of 85 percent or more, so whenever a first period class had 85 percent or more students in attendance for 10 days, the teacher provided a Mystery Motivator reward from one of four student-selected choices (three were inexpensive or involved a brief amount of time, and one was more expensive or involved more time). As inexpensive or limited-time choices, students selected things like the option to play board games or 10 minutes of free time to talk. Higher-cost, more time-consuming choices included things like a pizza party and a potluck party. The principal also recognized each class that met the goal by delivering a certificate, which was then displayed on the classroom window or door. As mentioned in Chapter 4, Challenger's attendance initiative resulted in an improvement in ADA of 8.4 percentage points (from 77.2 percent in 2015–2016 to 85.6 percent in 2016–2017). The first-period attendance chart (see Figure 5.6) and the repeated emphasis on regular attendance by first-period teachers were major components of this initiative.

Classroom Motivational Systems

Classroom systems can be implemented in the first period or hour of the day, in each class throughout the day, in a daily advisory period, or in homeroom. Individual teachers can design and implement them, or they can be part of a coordinated schoolwide effort with all teachers using the same system. This section provides examples and general descriptions of how to implement classroom-based motivational systems.

Here are some implementation models to consider.

- Provide a range of options for classroom motivational systems and allow individual teachers to decide whether their class would benefit from such a system. In this model, some teachers may choose not to implement a motivational system if attendance is not a problem with

FIGURE 5.6 **Challenger High School Attendance Chart**

Teacher: Ms. Enriques_____ Class period: ____1_____
Number of students enrolled: ___15_____ Record data at 8:00 a.m._____

Goal: __13__ students in class, on time (85 percent of students enrolled in class).
When our class meets this goal for 10 days, we will get the Mystery Motivator.
Term 1: September 2018

Special Notes: H = Holiday   TWD = Teacher Work Day   O = Other

# of Students Present	9/3	9/4	9/5	9/6	9/7	9/10	9/11	9/12	9/13	9/14
15										
14										
13										
12										
11										
10										
9										
8										
7										
6										
5										
4										
3										
2										
1										

their particular group of students. Other teachers may design, deliver, and monitor their own classroom systems. Provide opportunities for individual teachers to share their classroom systems and results with the rest of the teaching staff.

- Require that each teacher select one or more motivational systems for implementation, but allow each teacher to determine which one to use. Individual teachers design and deliver their own classroom system. Once a month have teachers report on the efficacy of their classroom systems and problem-solve possible improvements with the attendance team or with each other.

- Provide a range of options for classroom motivational systems, and have teachers vote in grade-level teams (or other logical teams based on your school organization) on which system they will use as a group. The groups design the system and create needed materials. Individual teachers deliver the system in their classroom and periodically share and problem-solve with the other teachers in the group. Groups of teachers periodically share their system and its results with the whole staff.

- Provide a range of options for classroom motivational systems, and have the whole teaching staff vote on which system to adopt in every classroom (see "Adopt a Plan" in Chapter 4, pp. 68–69). The team creates all materials for teachers and regularly collects data from teachers and testimonials on the results of the system and shares this information with the school community.

- The attendance team reviews options for classroom motivational systems and decides on one or more systems that will be used in every classroom. The team creates all materials for teachers and regularly collects data from teachers and testimonials on the system's effects to share with the school community. After one month, the team solicits staff feedback and reviews data on how the system is working to determine whether to continue the system, make adjustments, or use a different strategy.

Notice that these options range from those that provide the most teacher autonomy but also require the most teacher work time to those decided by the whole staff or the team, with groups of teachers or the team taking over the workload of creating procedures and materials. Consider the dynamics and politics of your staff when deciding which approach to use (e.g., staff commitment to initiative, preference for unity versus need for autonomy, staff communication and teaching styles, amount of time for staff to create and implement systems).

Daily classroom attendance graph. No matter which approach you choose, a graph showing daily classroom attendance can serve as an effective visual portrayal of how the initiative is going and—if results are trending in the right direction—a powerful motivator to continue the effort. Create a large poster for each teacher with a line graph or bar chart displaying the number of students in the class in attendance each day (see the example in Figure 5.7). For secondary teachers or elementary specials teachers who see multiple groups of students throughout the day, create a poster for each class period and assemble the posters into a flip chart using binder rings. Draw a goal line on the chart that is specific to each class based on the previous class attendance rate. The goal can be determined by looking at the average classroom attendance for at least three days before starting the system. Encourage teachers to set a goal that is reasonable and pushes the students without being too far out of their reach. In some classrooms with fairly good attendance, this may mean the goal is 100 percent of students present. In classes

FIGURE 5.7 **Graph of Daily Classroom Attendance**

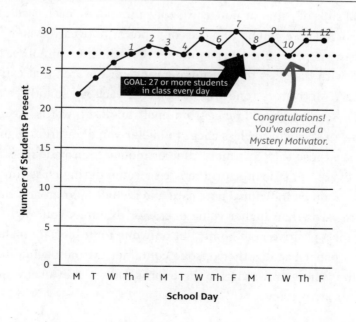

with poor attendance, the goal may be to have two or three more students in attendance than the current number (e.g., if the baseline average is 24 out of 30 students, set a goal of 27 students to start). As students succeed in meeting this goal, the teacher can gradually move the goal upward.

Posters should be displayed at the front of each classroom or in another highly visible classroom location. At the beginning of each day (or period in secondary school), the teacher counts and graphs the number of students in the room. Encourage teachers to show anticipation and enthusiasm for the system and to use this ritual to emphasize the importance of attendance for student success and the classroom culture, as well as to problem-solve with students when they are having difficulties meeting the goal.

Mystery Motivators. Enhance the system by using Mystery Motivators when students meet their goal for a certain number of days. Brainstorm possible classroom rewards with students. Create prize cards with one possible reward on each card. List a large number of no- or low-cost items in terms of money or time, a moderate number of medium-cost items or activities, and one high-cost item or activity. Determine the criterion for how many days the class needs to meet or exceed the goal to earn the reward. Use the general principle of providing the reinforcement relatively quickly at first (e.g., the reward is earned when the goal is met three times) and then increasing the number of days or the percentage that must be earned.

Classroom group contingency. This system can be used with a whole class or a small group of students. Write down the following numbers on individual slips of paper or note cards (one number on each card): 1, 2, 3, 3, 4, 4, 4, 5, 5, 5. There will be 10 pieces of paper or note cards when finished. Put them in a paper bag or other container that students cannot see through.

Work with the class to determine a range of rewards that can be used for Mystery Motivators (one will be selected each week and sealed in an envelope). Rewards should range from small, no-cost rewards like a positive note home or receiving a class cheer to higher-value rewards. Higher-value rewards are those that cost more time or money to provide (e.g., a special lunch delivered to students, or a movie or game during class time). Write each reward on an individual note card and include a far greater number of smaller rewards than higher-value ones. For example, you might prepare 10 cards for a positive note home, but only one for a special lunch. Put the cards in a paper bag or other opaque container. At the beginning of each week, blindly draw a reward from these cards and seal it in an envelope when all students are present.

FIGURE 5.8　**Teacher Log of Weekly Attendance**

Week of _____.

	Mon	Tues	Wed	Thurs	Fri	Total for Week
Monique Alvarez	X	X			X	3
Susie Anderson	X	X	X	X	X	5
Dustin Barnett	X	X	X	X	X	5
Jorie Baymont	X		X	X	X	4
Valerie Bjorquist	X	X	X	X	X	5
Dominique Chambers	X	X	X	X	X	5
Simon Covington	X					1
Sekou Camara	X	X	X	X	X	5
Destiny Favrou	X	X	X		X	4

Each morning, track attendance and praise all students for attending. You may wish to keep track on a weekly log or have students mark their own logs, filling in a box for each day they are present. If you plan to use a teacher log, we recommend that this be a private document, not a posted display, to ensure that no students are publicly shamed for poor attendance during a particular week. See Figure 5.8 for an example of a teacher chart and Figure 5.9 for a student chart.

On Friday morning, have one student select one of the numbered slips of paper from the bag. All students in the class whose attendance for the

FIGURE 5.9　**Student Log of Weekly Attendance**

Student Name _____

	Mon	Tues	Wed	Thurs	Fri	Total for Week
Week 1	X	X		X	X	4
Week 2	X	X	X	X	X	5
Week 3	X	X	X	X		4
Week 4						
Week 5						

week matched or exceeded the number drawn from the bag will receive the Mystery Motivator reward. Those who attended fewer days than the number drawn do not receive the reward.

Over time, you can make it more difficult for students to earn rewards by removing one of the lower-numbered note cards, such as a 2 or a 3, and replacing it with a higher-numbered note card, such as a 4 or a 5. Gradually removing the lower numbers makes it less likely that a student will earn the reward if she attends fewer days during the week. However, always keep the notecard with the number 1 so that even when a student misses four days at the beginning of the week, there is an incentive to attend on Friday. At the most advanced stage of the system, the note cards will read: 1, 5, 5, 5, 5, 5, 5, 5, 5, 5.

Monthly group contingency adaptation. Consider adapting the classroom group contingency procedure so that the Mystery Motivator is drawn once a month rather than once a week. The greater the attendance problems across a whole class, the more frequently rewards should be delivered; however, if attendance is generally fairly good or a weekly drawing is overwhelming, a monthly drawing might be preferable. In a 20-day month, the numbers on the notecards can be adapted to something like this: 10, 16, 18, 18, 19, 19, 19, 20, 20, 20. Remember to keep one number card relatively low so that even if students have highly problematic attendance during the first half or three-fourths of the month, they still have an incentive to attend for the remainder and win the reward.

Use Motivational Systems for Staff

One way to keep staff energized about the attendance initiative and to infuse some fun into their efforts is to provide one or more motivational systems for teachers or the whole staff. Here are some ideas.

Reward Teachers for Students' Attendance

Consider a motivational system that rewards teachers based on their classroom's attendance. For example, the school can reward the teacher whose class had the best attendance for the month or week, or the most improved attendance from one month to the next. Teachers can have their names entered into a raffle if their class met the ADA goal for the month or had improved attendance from one month to the next, or each time their class reaches its 10-day goal, if the school is using the whole-school classroom attendance system described on page 82.

Like the motivational systems for students, staff systems can use a Mystery Motivator approach, with numerous rewards that are low- or no-cost items or activities, some medium-cost rewards, and one or two high-value rewards. Possible rewards include the following:

- An article in the school newsletter about something positive in the teacher's classroom
- Permission for 10-minute late arrival or early departure during morning or afternoon prep time
- A hallway or classroom bulletin board for the class designed by an administrator or interventionist
- Coffee or tea drink of the teacher's choice delivered to the classroom
- Gift certificate for a massage or a restaurant meal
- VIP or reserved parking spot for a day or week
- Movie pass
- Gift card from a local coffee chain
- A student to help carry bags to or from car for a day or week
- Skip the day's lunch duty
- Free lunch in cafeteria
- Lunch or dessert made by an administrator or colleague
- Free school T-shirt
- Opportunity to name the next school spirit day (e.g., Dr. Seuss day, favorite cartoon day, Disney day)

Conduct Periodic Self-Reflection Activities Related to Staff Absences

In some schools, frequent and excessive staff absences can contribute to a message that regular attendance (and even school itself) is not important. The attendance team and administrator will need to tread carefully when holding discussions about staff absences to avoid implying that staff should not take sick days or use other allocated absence times as needed. However, it may be important to have periodic staff reflection times so that staff can evaluate whether their absences are contributing to a negative attendance culture and to ensure that absences are used wisely and appropriately.

Consider the following activities:

- Ask staff to brainstorm the negative effects when teachers and other staff members are not at school. Brainstorming and sharing lists of negative effects can be validating for staff, enabling them to understand their importance in the functioning of the school and the well-being of their students. For example, staff may identify the following:
  - o Effects on instruction (e.g., even the best substitutes cannot provide the same quality and continuity of academic instruction)
  - o Increased difficulties for students who rely on relationships (e.g., students with anxiety or behavioral deficits are likely to struggle with substitutes and may even exhibit increased absenteeism because certain adults are not consistently present)
  - o Less planning time for regular instructional activities because of prep time needed to plan for days when the teacher is absent
- Provide an individualized absence report each term or semester for staff members and have them reflect on which attendance category they would be in (e.g., Regular Attendance, At-Risk Attendance, Chronic Absence).
- Include whole-group feedback or data on staff attendance at staff meetings, especially if improvements have occurred.
- Provide one or more staff motivational systems to encourage regular staff attendance (e.g., each month, provide raffle tickets to staff members in attendance on random days; then raffle off items or activities to staff members at the end of the month).

Some of the motivational systems described for students can be adapted to provide a fun way to encourage staff members to be at school as regularly as possible. These staff systems are analogous to the various motivational and feedback systems that hospitals use to encourage doctors and nurses to wash their hands. Although all doctors and nurses know that it is critical to wash their hands, the Centers for Disease Control and Prevention has indicated that healthcare providers wash their hands less than half the number of times they should. To address this problematic trend, hospitals do things like publishing a goal for handwashing rates, measuring compliance and publicly posting the collective handwashing rates of their staff, and randomly providing rewards to staff who are "caught" washing their hands. In schools, staff members may know the importance of being in school every day possible, but gentle, playful reminders can be effective to encourage the best staff attendance rates possible.

When you implement these motivational and feedback systems with staff, be extremely careful that procedures do not embarrass staff members who are absent or imply they should not take days of absence that are allocated to them. Rather, design procedures that honor staff members for how important they are to the students and the school system and that provide a fun incentive for attendance. For example, a competition to highlight the grade level with the best monthly teacher attendance might be appropriate, whereas a public posting of individual teachers' attendance and a reward for best attendance would be inappropriate.

Like student absences, some teacher absences follow a pattern. You can look at the previous year's staff absences by month and send out a memo before problematic months (e.g., if staff absences were high in March, send a memo in February with reminders about the importance of staff attendance, tips for increasing attendance, and information about one or more staff motivational systems).

It's worth repeating that with any strategies, ensure that you maintain confidentiality so that no individual can be identified or targeted during the activities. The tone should be encouraging and respectful rather than punitive. The goal is not to discourage or punish staff for using absences they are entitled to, but to encourage them to recognize their importance to the school community and be present whenever reasonable and possible.

Maintain Communication About Attendance Efforts

To sustain the momentum built by the initial campaign kickoff, the school must provide ongoing communication about the school's attendance goals, acknowledgment of successes, and communication about difficulties. Chapter 7 provides in-depth examples of effective ways to communicate and engage with families and the community, but here we present a few preliminary suggestions.

Ensure that staff, students, and families regularly receive information about the school's goals as well as current rates of ADA and percentages of students in the Regular Attendance, At-Risk Attendance, Chronic Absence, and Severe Chronic Absence categories. Provide updates to the community as appropriate.

Although it is important to emphasize the ultimate goal of 100 percent of students in the Regular Attendance category, it is also important to set reasonable interim goals (e.g., if 65 percent of students are in the Regular Attendance category in the first two months of school, advertise a goal of 75 to 80 percent of students in that category for the following two months). When a goal is reached or noticeable improvements occur, communicate and celebrate this accomplishment with staff, students, and families. When consistent problems or trends are noticed, they should be communicated as well.

Ongoing communication about attendance efforts can be presented in a variety of formats and media. Here are some examples:

- Regular updates at monthly staff meetings
- An article in the school newsletter (some schools have dedicated article space, such as the right column of the first page, where attendance updates, goals, and tips are provided each month)
- Memos to staff
- Lessons for students created by the attendance team using presentation software for all classes and grades
- Letters (e-mail messages, snail mail, or as a form of homework) or robocall updates to parents
- Blasts on social media and school website about successes, goals, or current rates of attendance

Remember that the more widespread absenteeism problems are throughout your school, the more the school should strive for frequent communication through a variety of media with all stakeholders—staff, students, families, and community.

■　■　■　■　■

The strategies described in this chapter are some of the most powerful for building enthusiasm and momentum for your attendance efforts. We cannot underestimate the importance of a fun and welcoming atmosphere for staff and students, which can be built in part through the motivational and other strategies described. When used along with the strategies in Chapter 6 ("Teaching Students About the Importance of Regular Attendance"), we solidify students' understanding of why attendance is critical to their success and help ensure that they want to be in school each day.

■ ■ ■ ■ ■

Outline of Tasks for Creating and Sustaining an Attendance Campaign

Use the following outline as a quick reminder of the tasks involved in creating and sustaining an attendance campaign.

Conduct activities to kick off the attendance campaign.

- Indicate how and when you will create a title or slogan (e.g., staff brainstorming session or student competition after assembly).
- Indicate the initial strategies to be used to generate enthusiasm for your attendance campaign (e.g., publicity at back-to-school or parent night or letter and attendance tracker sent home).

Use schoolwide and classroom motivational systems.

- Select one or more schoolwide or classroom motivational systems and make notes about what is needed for implementation.

Maintain communication about attendance efforts with staff, students, families, and the community.

- Indicate ways that you plan to update stakeholders about attendance goals and data.
- Select dates when information will be shared with the following stakeholders:
  - Staff
  - Students
  - Families
  - Community (as appropriate)

Teaching Students About the Importance of Regular Attendance

Why should we teach students about the importance of regular attendance? The answer is simple: doing so is easy, it's cheap, and it may significantly reduce the problem! Many students simply do not understand that their attendance is a critical factor that can influence their success or failure in class, in school, and in their jobs or career. In a survey of students in grades 8 through 12 who reported skipping school a few times a month or more, only 18 percent of students believed it was "very likely" that they would personally fall behind in their classes if they skipped once a week (Get Schooled Foundation, 2012). Many students do not understand that only two days a month could set them on a path toward dropping out. Brundage, Castillo, and Batsche (2017) found that only 43 percent of students who were chronically absent recalled or reported levels of absenteeism that would place them in the Chronic Absence category, indicating that many chronically absent students may not know they have problematic levels of absenteeism. In addition, 55.2 percent of chronically absent students believed they had levels of absence similar to those of their peers, overestimating other students' levels of absenteeism.

In this chapter we provide tools and strategies to help your students understand that attendance is a critical variable for passing classes, making meaningful connections with staff and students, and graduating with the skills they need to be successful in whatever goals they hold for their future.

Teach Formal Lessons About Attendance

All students should receive some general information emphasizing the importance of attendance and teaching them about the goal of every student having regular attendance. Depending on the magnitude of attendance problems in your school, these lessons may occur as infrequently as a few times a year to as frequently as weekly or daily. Lessons should be relatively short (5 to 15 minutes) and age appropriate, and help students understand that success depends on being in school regularly.

Determine When to Formally Emphasize Attendance

Teachers typically deliver attendance lessons to their classes. In some cases, however, you may wish to have the attendance team or specific personnel (e.g., counselor or social worker) rotate through classes to deliver lessons. This approach is recommended whenever content is highly sensitive, if you want to ensure a consistent message across all classrooms, or when you want to provide students the opportunity to connect with interventionists. For example, if a lesson covers seeking out school supports when absenteeism is related to emotional or health issues and you hope to encourage students to connect with support services, it may make sense for the counselors or school nurse to deliver these lessons. As you create your lesson schedule, determine which lessons will be delivered by teachers and which will be delivered by other staff who rotate through classes. These decisions will affect how you schedule the attendance lessons.

When teachers deliver the lessons in elementary school, it usually makes sense to give them discretion to teach the lesson at whatever time makes the most sense during a particular day. Provide the lesson in advance and let teachers know that they will be expected to deliver the lesson on a specific date.

Secondary schools offer a few options for when teachers can deliver attendance lessons. An advisory or homeroom period is a logical time. If your school has no advisory or homeroom period, or that period is already being used for other content, plan for lessons to be delivered during a specific period or subject that rotates across time. For example, in Week 1, all first-period teachers deliver the attendance lesson; in Week 2, all second-period teachers deliver the lesson, and so on. In this way, no individual period or subject is overly affected by the lessons, and all students receive the same information.

Put in place periodic accountability measures, such as random spot-checks of student understanding, to ensure that all teachers are implementing the lessons. If any teachers are resistant to delivering lessons, determine ways to increase staff engagement with the attendance initiative, as described in Chapter 4.

Determine Who Will Develop Lessons

In general, the attendance team develops lessons; however, you may periodically engage other stakeholders to help. Consider the following options:

- Have all teachers participate in lesson development during a staff meeting. Divide teachers into small groups and have each small group create one 10- to 15-minute lesson.
- Have a different grade-level team of teachers take responsibility for creating a lesson plan for the whole school each month.
- Allow a student task force to develop one or more lessons with staff guidance.
- Assign a particular day when teachers can design their own content-focused lesson.

Design Effective Lessons

Lessons can take many formats, including stories, chants, lectures, modeling, filling out T-charts, role-play, examination of analogous problems, and discussion. Lessons should have a specific focus and goals, and use techniques common to good instruction. When appropriate, include the following elements in lesson plans:

- Rationale and objectives
- Active engagement techniques (e.g., think-pair-share, choral response, written response)
- Structure based on model, lead, test
- Role-play
- Opportunities for repeated practice
- Immediate positive and corrective feedback
- Assessment of student understanding

Figures 6.1 through 6.3 provide examples of attendance lessons that you can offer teachers as examples of what they can do in their classrooms.

FIGURE 6.1 **Lesson on Ways to Overcome Attendance Obstacles**

Objectives

- Students will explain ways to overcome obstacles that make it difficult to attend school.

- Students will summarize cause-and-effect relationships with absenteeism: absenteeism increases risks of dropping out; dropping out decreases future opportunities.

Procedures

1. In small groups or as a whole class, have students brainstorm responses to the following questions:
   - What would you do with $250,000?
   - What would you do with $1,000,000?

2. Introduce the following information:
   - A high school graduate makes, on average, almost $250,000 more over a lifetime than someone who drops out of high school.
   - A college graduate makes, on average, $1,000,000 more over a lifetime than a high school graduate.
   - (If time permits, present additional information about detrimental outcomes related to dropping out of high school.)
   - Missing even two days per month makes it much more difficult to graduate. One study found that students who are chronically absent are 7.4 times more likely to drop out than peers with regular attendance.

3. Have students share things that make it difficult for students to attend. Keep the discussion general so that no student feels pressured to share personal situations, but provide opportunities for students to share more personal examples (e.g., through written responses) with the teacher if desired.

4. Discuss with students and have them generate ideas for the following questions:
   - What can you do to overcome these difficulties?
   - What can we (the school, your family, community services, etc.) do to help you overcome these difficulties?

5. Have students complete an exit ticket summarizing how absenteeism can lead to decreased opportunities in the future. Leave space for students to indicate personal obstacles that they did not feel comfortable sharing with the class.

FIGURE 6.2 **Social Story Lesson**

Note: This lesson is most appropriate for students with disabilities and students in early childhood and primary grades (PreK through Grade 2).

Objectives

- Students will state that attendance is important and they should come to school each day when they are not sick.
- Students will participate in a classroom ritual for entry or exit.

Procedures

Step 1. At the beginning or end of each day (or both), recite one line of the social story shown in Step 2; then have students repeat the line using a choral response. Repeat for the remainder of the social story.

Step 2. Make classroom posters of the social story and provide personalized copies for students to illustrate, color, and take home.

I'm a very important person,
And school is very important.
I come to school every day
That I'm not sick.

When I come to school,
I learn a lot of things.
We have important work to do.
My friends and teachers miss me when I'm gone.

I come to school every day
That I'm not sick.

Design Content-Area Lessons

The following are samples of ideas for how to incorporate an attendance focus in content-area classes:

- In health class, provide lessons connecting hygiene and healthy lifestyle choices to attendance patterns in school and work.
- In English or language arts class, have students write sentences, paragraphs, or persuasive essays on why attendance is important.

FIGURE 6.3 **Analogous Problem Lesson**

Objectives

- Students will discuss why experts in any field continue to show up to practice, work, or professional development opportunities.
- Students compare benefits of attending school versus missing school.

Procedures

1. For the analogous problem, select a topic of high interest to students (e.g., football, music, gymnastics, theater).

2. Place a T-chart on the board and provide copies for students, as shown in this example (replace the topic as appropriate):

Why do famous football players show up for practice? Consider what happens to a football player who shows up as compared to one who doesn't show up for practice.

Player who shows up	Player who doesn't show up

3. Have students do a think-pair-share to complete the T-chart.
   a. Think: Have students complete the T-chart on their own. (3 minutes)
   b. Pair: Have students share their responses with a partner. Have each student record the partner's best ideas. (3 minutes)
   c. Share: Randomly call on students to share their partner's best idea. Record responses on the board. (3 minutes)

Why do famous football players show up for practice? Consider what happens to a football player who shows up as compared to one who doesn't show up for practice.

Player who shows up	Player who doesn't show up
• Gets stronger	• Loses skills and strength
• Pleases teammates and coach	• Lets down team and coach
• Gets more playing time	• Gets benched, possible suspension, or fired from team

(continued)

FIGURE 6.3 *(continued)*

4. Have students reflect and discuss how the items on their T-chart and on the board are similar to what happens to a student who shows up regularly to school in comparison with a student who is frequently absent.

   a. Provide one or two examples: "When a famous football player shows up to practice, he gets stronger. But if the player doesn't come, he's going to lose skills and strength over time. This is similar to a student who comes to school and strengthens skills in reading, math, and other subjects through regular practice. If a student doesn't come to school, over time he's likely to fall behind, and he might even lose some of the skills and strengths he already has."

   b. Have students talk in pairs about other responses on their T-chart that could relate to attendance in school, and have them circle items they can share with the class.

   c. Have students share with the whole class the responses that relate to school attendance and explain why they are relevant.

- In math class, when students are learning about graphing, percentages, and other related mathematical concepts, have them work with the school's data or data from research studies on attendance.

- In finance or math class, have students calculate pay per hour for a variety of jobs, then calculate lost wages based on days absent.

- In social studies or history class, discuss what would have happened if historical figures had not shown up on particularly important days.

- In science class, during lessons on plant growth, have students discuss or experiment with how attending to or not attending to plants would affect the growth of the plants, and compare this to student growth in school.

Informally Emphasize Attendance

One of the best ways to create a culture of attendance is for staff to emphasize the importance of attendance in many subtle and frequent ways. These range from staff greeting students by name each day to welcoming students back after absences to setting up informal procedures to contact students when they have been absent. Although teachers may have the most direct contact with students and should use the following strategies, we recommend also encouraging other staff (e.g., interventionists, administrators, lunchroom supervisors and chefs, custodians) to find ways to connect with students and emphasize the importance of being in school regularly. Provide periodic reminders to staff about ways that they can informally infuse an attendance message throughout interactions with students.

The following strategies are meaningful for all students, but they are especially important for students who are at risk or have histories of chronic absenteeism, disengagement, or behavioral or academic struggles in school.

Have Staff Greet Students and Welcome Them After an Absence

Staff members may underestimate the power of simple greetings and saying to a student, "We missed you," "I'm so glad you are back," or "Is everything OK? I noticed you've been gone the last few days." Welcoming students by name each day and providing follow-up when a student has been absent can go a long way toward making the student feel noticed and appreciated. It also provides a subtle accountability mechanism, as a student will tend to naturally respond to a teacher or adult whom the student respects and admires about the reasons for the absence.

Encourage teachers to greet students by name at the door when they enter the room. Some teachers add a personalized handshake or other greeting that can increase the likelihood that the interaction is meaningful for the student. Encourage teachers to review attendance charts so that they can make a point to greet students who were absent the previous day.

Jessica recalls that when she was in elementary school, everyone's favorite staff member was Martha, the cafeteria and recess supervisor. Whenever someone returned after an absence, Martha always came up to that student in the lunch line to say, "You were absent yesterday and I missed you!" Not only did she know who was absent, but she also made all students feel like she cared if they were gone and looked forward to seeing them when they came back to school. Jessica found out later that before lunch each day, Martha would look at the previous day's attendance and identify students who were absent so that she could make a point of greeting them when they returned. Her simple act made all students feel noticed and valued.

Encourage Staff to Call Students When They Have Been Absent More Than One Day

When a student has been absent for two or more days in a row or during a one-month period, it is valuable for the student's teacher and other staff members who the student is connected with (e.g., counselor or classified staff member) to call and say something like, "We miss you when you are gone and hope you will be back in class soon." These calls do not need to be lengthy or involved but should send a simple message that the student is missed when absent. This gesture is especially important in middle and high school, where students may feel that no one notices or cares when they are absent. In fact, the Get Schooled Foundation (2012) reported that 32 percent of students who skipped school stated that adults in the school (teachers, administrators, and attendance officers) rarely or never notice that they are gone, and an additional 32 percent said that adults in school notice only sometimes. All students should feel that someone notices and cares whenever they are not in school.

A good example of the importance of this effort comes from Jessica's own high school experience. As a fairly savvy student, she knew her school's attendance policy. It stated that after seven *unexcused* absences in a semester, a student's grade would be reduced by one letter grade for each subsequent absence. Jessica was a martial artist and sometimes skipped classes to train and work out. She started keeping track of her unexcused absences, marking a tally in the corner of the divider in her binder for each class period. She made sure to never go above the seven absences for any given class, and her attendance never triggered any sort of intervention or concern from the school. Considering that she had excused absences as well, her attendance record would have shown that she was chronically absent for most of high school. Luckily, she was able to compensate academically; however, she wonders how much more she would have learned if she hadn't missed so much school!

The point of this story is that no teacher, administrator, or other school staff member ever asked her where she had been the previous day, much less said they would call her parents or initiate other intervention efforts if these problematic attendance patterns continued. She highly respected her teachers, and if any one of them had asked her where she had been, she would have never skipped that class again. She would not have wanted to lie to them or have to tell them she skipped the class. The truth was, she thought it didn't matter if she missed some school, and no one ever told her otherwise.

When a student exhibits a pattern of problematic absenteeism, more in-depth discussions and phone calls may be warranted. See Chapter 10 for early-stage classroom interventions such as phone calls home and planned discussion that can be implemented by the teacher or other school personnel.

Have Staff Encourage Students to Call One Another When a Student Has Been Absent

In some classrooms, teachers institute a buddy or small-group system that connects each student with one to three other students. When students are absent, their partner or team can ask to call them to tell them they are missed and encourage them to come back as soon as possible. Provide possible talking points for students so that they know how to provide encouragement in positive ways (e.g., "I hope you get better soon!" "We will be thinking about you until you come back!").

■ ■ ■ ■ ■

In this chapter we have emphasized formally teaching students about the importance of regular attendance. Consider how to distribute lessons across the year and in subsequent years so that the attendance initiative and the school's goals for regular attendance for all students remain relevant across time. Also consider ways to reenergize staff to informally emphasize the importance of attendance with students (and families) throughout the school year. Note that information that is taught in formal lessons and informally emphasized with students throughout the year should also be conveyed to families. Chapter 7 provides strategies for communicating about your attendance initiative with families and the community. As you work through Chapters 6 and 7, consider which information that you plan to teach to students should also be taught and reinforced with parents. In Chapter 8, you will learn how to tailor aspects of your schoolwide plan to address causes of absenteeism that are common in your school. As you work through Chapter 8, consider formal lessons for students that teach about how to avoid common barriers and how to address other common causes of absenteeism such as bullying or academic concerns.

■ ■ ■ ■ ■

Summary of Tasks for Teaching Students About the Importance of Regular Attendance

Use the following outline as a quick reminder of the tasks involved in teaching students about the importance of regular attendance.

Teach formal lessons about attendance to all students.

- Develop a schedule for when lessons will be delivered and determine who will deliver them (e.g., teachers, interventionists).

- Determine who will create lessons and provide information about recommended elements to incorporate into lesson design (e.g., rationale, active engagement).

- Create and implement attendance lessons and archive all materials for future use.

Have staff informally emphasize attendance with all students.

- Determine how you will initially train staff; then provide ongoing support and reminders about informally emphasizing the importance of attendance.

- Determine which of the following strategies you will share with staff and when:
  - Greeting students by name
  - Welcoming students back after an absence
  - Calling students when they have been absent more than a day
  - Setting up procedures for students to call one another when a peer is absent

Enhancing Family and Community Involvement

Absenteeism is not a problem that schools can tackle alone. Because the negative effects have an impact on all stakeholders, building a culture of attendance requires the combined efforts of everyone, including families and community members. In this chapter we provide tools for educating families and the community about the importance of attendance, and recommendations for empowering the family and community to work as partners to tackle issues that lead to absenteeism.

Educate Families and Provide Tools to Improve Attendance

We sometimes hear educators (especially in elementary school) make statements like this: "We can't do anything to change his attendance. It's a parent problem, and his parents just don't care about school or his regular attendance." These educators feel disempowered to address attendance issues.

Although a few families may truly not care, the good news is that a far greater number are simply operating off misinformation or don't have adequate tools, skills, and supports to help their child attend school regularly. For example, the Boost-Up Campaign—an antidropout effort sponsored by the U.S. Army and the Ad Council (2015)—interviewed low-income parents of students with poor attendance. They found that most parents wanted a better life for their children and saw high school graduation as critical to that goal. They found that parents held many misconceptions about attendance. Among other findings, parents did not make the connection between attendance in elementary or middle school and graduation; they said they would get stricter about attendance when students were in high school. The parents also viewed skipping school as a problem but did not realize that problems could occur with excused absences as well as unexcused ones. The following section provides strategies to dispel these misconceptions.

Launch the Attendance Initiative with Families

As you begin your attendance initiative, consider how best to generate enthusiasm within the parent population of your school. In most cases, using multiple formats and methods for connecting with families will increase the likelihood that parents will understand the importance of attendance and the school's goals. As much as possible, provide materials and information in families' first languages and invite interpreters to events that parents will attend. Select from the following menu of activities or design your own activities to get parents involved.

Make a presentation about the attendance campaign at back-to-school night. Select information from Chapter 1 to share with families, or search for studies relevant to the student population in your school. Highlight attendance data from the previous year and share information about the school's current goals. It may also be useful to have staff write anecdotal notes about how absenteeism negatively affects their classrooms and to share a summary of these statements with families.

Blast information on social media. If your school has a social media account that parents follow, send out information a few weeks before the launch of the attendance initiative that previews the start of the campaign or provides teasers about information to come (e.g., "In two days, the Bulldogs will launch a new campaign that may be the biggest thing yet for helping our students be successful! Stay tuned!").

Publish a feature story in the school newspaper. Use the front page of the school newspaper to present an in-depth story about the importance of attendance, the school's data and goals, and ways that parents and students can work with the school to improve attendance.

Send home letters introducing the attendance campaign. Provide information about the campaign in the family's first language and send it home through the mail as well as with students to increase the likelihood that parents receive the information.

Create visuals and post them throughout the school. Create posters announcing the campaign and the school's goals and place them in prominent locations throughout the school where parents are likely to see them (e.g., on the school reader board, in the front office, on sign posts in parent pick-up and drop-off sections of the parking lot and adjoining streets).

Contact local media and ask them to cover the launch of the campaign. Reach out to local television stations, radio stations, and newspapers that provide information to the community. Share the rationale for the attendance campaign and how it can improve outcomes for students and the community, and invite the organization to interview staff and students or show footage of the attendance assembly.

School Resource Officer John Calvert of Jackson County, Kansas, is influential in his schools because of the positive and lasting relationships he builds with all students. He extended that influence by using the power of the media to inform his community about the importance of school attendance. Officer John convinced the local sheriff's department to pay part of the fee (and paid the rest himself) to attend a Safe & Civil Schools session on school attendance. Officer John left the conference fired up and immediately began figuring out ways to reach out to his community and help build a culture of attendance. He went to local news organizations and within two weeks, multiple television stations ran stories that included interviews with him about his goal of eliminating chronic absenteeism in the county's schools. During the interviews, he spoke about the importance of attendance and his mission of ensuring that all students know they will be missed if they are absent. He said, "Hopefully, in the kid's head, he goes, 'Oh, man, Officer John knew that I was gone. Officer John will know if I'm not there.'" (You can view one of the stories at www.wibw.com/content/news/Salute-the-Badge-Jackson -County-SRO-puts-rhythm-into-school-safety-440426703.html.)

Invite parents to events. If your school is conducting assemblies, awards ceremonies, or other events related to the attendance campaign, invite parents, as appropriate. For example, Barnes Elementary School in Kelso, Washington, invites all families to the Big Bear BBQ, an end-of-year celebration to honor kids and families who have maintained regular attendance throughout the year. All families are invited to come and enjoy hot dogs, hamburgers, and games, and students with 95 percent or better attendance across the year receive special awards and are entered in prize drawings. The school also invites prominent community members such as the mayor, police officers, physicians, and church officials.

Provide Ongoing Communication About Attendance Efforts

Parents should receive regular communications from the school, including information about both the overall school attendance for the student body as well as their child's attendance. Parents should know exactly how many absences their child has accrued at any point during the school year—and the corresponding attendance category. Consider the following ways to provide ongoing communication.

Send home color-coded letters indicating each student's current attendance rate. Create form letters that can be sent home at least once every two months to indicate a student's current attendance category (Regular Attendance, At-Risk Attendance, Chronic Absence, Severe Chronic Absence). Print each letter on colored paper that corresponds to the level of risk (e.g., green for Regular, yellow for At-Risk, red for Chronic, dark red for Severe Chronic), and tailor the message accordingly. (See Figures 7.1 and 7.2 for sample wording for a Regular Attendance letter and a Chronic Absence letter, respectively.) To increase the value of this letter, have each student fill in the number of absences and the attendance percentage before it is sent home, and include a printout of the student's attendance record.

Place copies of the color-coded letters in student files during conferences and make student attendance a standard talking point. Provide teachers with a list of all their students, sorted by class period, in each of the attendance categories. Create a form letter similar to those depicted in Figures 7.1 and 7.2, and have teachers place the appropriate letters in student files before conferences. To prepare teachers to discuss students' attendance rates with parents, you can provide a list of recommendations for conducting such conversations. Figure 7.3 shows a sample memo from a principal to staff.

Send home periodic updates about schoolwide attendance rates using a variety of media. Use letters home, robocalls, social media, the school website, and other easy methods of communication to inform families about progress related to the attendance initiative. Consider dedicating a regular space in the school newsletter to a monthly attendance column. Provide schoolwide attendance updates (e.g., ADA for the month and year, percentage of students in the Regular Attendance, At-Risk Attendance, and Chronic Absence categories), the school's goals for attendance, and acknowledgment of individuals, classes, or the whole school. Communication might also contain information on any new motivational systems that the school will implement and tips for parents on addressing common problems that contribute to absenteeism.

FIGURE 7.1 **Parent Letter for Regular Attendance**

Dear parent of _____:

We want to congratulate you and your student for maintaining regular attendance (missing no more than 5 percent of days in the current year)! So far this year, your student has had _____ absences, representing an attendance rate of _____ percent. We know that it is not always easy to get to school each day, and we appreciate your efforts to set your student up for success. You are also helping the school reach our goal of 97 percent Average Daily Attendance. Keep up the good work!

We know that students who miss even a few days each month are at far greater risk of academic failure and dropping out than students who attend regularly. By ensuring that your student has fewer than nine absences in a year, you are helping your student have the best chances in life. If you encounter difficulties that put your child at risk of missing too much school, please feel free to contact the school counselor, Joan Ndogo, at 555-1234 for assistance. We are happy to work with you to help your student maintain regular attendance.

Sincerely,

Aaron Chan, Principal

FIGURE 7.2 **Parent Letter for Chronic Absence**

Dear parent of _____:

We want to inform you of our concerns about your student's current attendance rate and reach out to see how we can partner with you to improve your student's attendance. So far this year, your student has had _____ absences, representing an attendance rate of _____ percent.

This level of absenteeism triggers concerns, as we know that students who miss even a few days each month are at far greater risk of academic failure and dropping out than students who attend regularly. Students who miss 10 percent or more of school may have difficulty with academic content, struggle to maintain positive relationships with peers or adults in the school, and have high rates of disengagement and school failure over time.

We know that it is not always easy to get to school each day, and many situations can cause a student to be absent from school. However, we also know that with a partnership between the school and families, we can work together to find solutions to many of the barriers and situations that prevent students from being in school. Please contact the school counselor, Joan Ndogo, at 555-1234, or Sergio Garcia, our behavior specialist, at 555-1235 for assistance. We are happy to work with you to help your student maintain regular attendance. If we do not hear from you and attendance continues to be a concern, school personnel will be in touch to problem solve and work out a plan.

We thank you for your efforts to help your student attend school regularly. By working to ensure your student is in school every day that he or she is not seriously ill, you are helping your student have the best chances in school and in life.

Sincerely,

Aaron Chan, Principal

FIGURE 7.3 **Memo to Staff for Conferences**

DATE: October 3
TO: All Staff
FROM: Aaron Chan, Principal
SUBJECT: Upcoming family conferences and absenteeism initiative

Conferences are a great opportunity for us to remind parents about the importance of regular attendance for their students and for our school community. We have given you a list of your students in each of the attendance categories (Regular Attendance, At-Risk Attendance, Chronic Absence, Severe Chronic Absence) and color-coded letters that you can put in each student's file (green for Regular, yellow for At-Risk, red for Chronic, and dark red for Severe Chronic). As you conduct conferences with parents, consider the following talking points for students in each of the categories:

- Congratulate parents of students with *regular attendance* and encourage them to keep getting their students to school regularly. Remind them that the fewer absences their child has during a year, the greater the likelihood of success. They are giving their students a foundation that supports success.

- For students with *at-risk attendance*, let parents know that the student's attendance is below what is recommended for the student to have the best possible chances of success in school. Say something like this:

> Johnny has missed five days in the first three months of school, which puts him in the At-Risk Attendance category. We know that students in this category may experience negative outcomes if absenteeism continues, such as lower grades, disengagement from adults or peers, and other struggles in school.

Ask parents if there is anything they need help with or any way the school can help in getting the student to school. Provide contact information for personnel in the school who can assist if parents need support. Say something like this:

> We know that it's not always easy getting to school each day and that many families face barriers that may prevent a student from being in school. If you have any of these concerns and would like to talk to me or someone else at the school, we hope to assist in any way we can. If you would like to get in

(continued)

FIGURE 7.3 **(continued)**

touch with someone, here is my e-mail address. We've also included the phone numbers and e-mail addresses of our counselor and social worker in this letter.

Conclude this portion of the conference by indicating that you look forward to having the student in class every day.

- With parents of students who are *chronically absent* or are *severely chronically absent*, attempt to strike a supportive and nonjudgmental tone, but indicate that the student's absences are a concern. Here's an example:

Cinda and Darrell, we see that Martin has missed seven days of school in the first three months, which means he has been chronically absent. We are very concerned when a student misses this much school because there are significant risks such as course failure, disengagement, and dropping out. We also miss him when he is absent! We would love to work with you to problem solve and figure out the best way to improve his attendance.

Highlight the information about personnel in the school who are available to provide support and who will be in touch if absenteeism continues to be a problem. Here's an example:

We know that it's not always easy getting to school each day and that many families face barriers that may prevent a student from being in school. If you would like to talk to me or someone else at the school about any concerns that make it difficult for Martin to attend regularly, we hope to assist in any way we can. If you would like to get in touch with someone, here is my e-mail address. We've also included the phone numbers and e-mail addresses of our counselor and social worker in this letter. Please know that we view Martin's attendance as a critical factor in his success. If the current attendance pattern continues and we haven't heard from you, we will follow up with you and with Martin to see what we can all do to solve this issue.

Increase Communication with Families During Problematic Times of Year

Certain times of year are predictably problematic. For example, absenteeism is higher in most schools during the weeks before and after winter and spring breaks. Your data may indicate that other times of year are problematic for your school. Before these times of year, increase communication with families and encourage regular attendance. For example, in the weeks leading up to winter break, use the following strategies to increase the likelihood that parents will send their children to school.

Use a variety of media (e.g., letters home, social media, robocalls) to remind families that teachers will be teaching right up until the vacation starts and will resume teaching on the first day after the break.

Use radio or television public service announcements (PSAs) to emphasize the importance of attending school every day before and after a break. When possible, have a local, state, or national celebrity record the PSA to increase family and student interest in the message. For example, if you have a professional sports team in your area, you might contact the organization to see if one or more players would be willing to record a 30-second message encouraging students to be in school before and after vacations. Some schools contacted radio and television stations, ready to pay for air time, but then learned that the PSA would run free of charge when they described the intent of the message, simply because the stations believed in the importance of kids being in school every day! Attendance Works (attendanceworks.org) provides a wealth of tools educators can use as part of their attendance initiatives. Figure 7.4 is a sample 30-second public service announcement from Attendance Works.

FIGURE 7.4 **Sample Public Service Announcement**

This holiday season, the best gift you can give your child is a good education. And the best place to get an education is in school. It's tempting to extend your vacation a few days, but remember, those count as absences. Just a few missed days here and there, even if they're excused, can add up to too much lost learning time. So, make sure your child is in school every day, right up until vacation starts. Our teachers will be teaching, and our students will be learning.

Source: From "The Gift of Attendance: Messaging Attendance in the Holiday Season," 2012. Retrieved from www.attendanceworks.org/wordpress/wp-content/uploads/2012/08/giftofattendance2.pdf. Copyright © 2012 Attendance Works. Used with permission.

Send home information and provide lessons at parent nights and school celebrations about the lost learning time that results when families extend holiday vacations in the days before or after winter and spring breaks. See Figure 7.5 for a lesson that can be taught to families about the detrimental effects of extending school vacations.

Although extending vacations around the holidays or spring break is an extremely common problem across many schools and districts, the causes can vary widely. At one national conference we conducted, two participants shared very different causes and approaches to addressing the problem. One principal indicated that families in his community were extremely wealthy, so many were going on ski vacations and trips to foreign countries. These parents wanted to leave early or come back late so they could avoid high-volume travel times. Teaching the lesson in Figure 7.5, however, was effective in helping many families choose to contain their trip within the school's vacation schedule because these parents were highly invested in getting their students as prepared as possible for competitive colleges. Another principal indicated that his school had a similar problem with extended absences around the holiday vacation time but mainly because a large portion of the student body consisted of children from immigrant families from South American countries. These families went to South America to see everyone and partake in important family celebrations. In this case, the school and community determined that an appropriate solution would be to accommodate these families by altering the break schedule by lengthening the winter break and shortening the summer break to accommodate the standard days in school. The point to remember is that you need to be considerate of sensitive matters (e.g., financial, familial, and religious) as well as cultural considerations as you consider what information to send home or how to deliver information and lessons to parents.

Encourage or require teachers to provide high-level, high-quality instruction in the weeks before and after breaks. Help teachers understand that although it is tempting to do activities with lower instructional value, doing so leads to significant lost learning time and perpetuates the cycle of students being absent before and after vacations because they feel they are not missing anything important. Increase the frequency of administrator walk-throughs and publicly acknowledge classes where meaningful instructional activities are taking place. For example, send out a daily e-mail message the week before and after break to acknowledge high-quality instruction going on in specific teachers' classrooms.

FIGURE 7.5 **Lesson for Families About Extending Holiday Vacations**

Objective

Parents will calculate the amount of lost learning time that occurs across a student's school career when the student misses school the week before and after a break.

Procedures

1. Explain to parents that many students are missing one or more days of school the week before and the week after a school vacation. When possible, provide information about the average number of students who miss one or more days during these times in your school, and break that down into the average number of students missing in each classroom. For example, "Across our student body, we had 92 students who missed one or more days of school in the week before winter break. That means we had 4 to 5 students missing from every single classroom."

2. Describe the following vicious cycle:

   a. When large numbers of students are missing from a class, a teacher is faced with the difficult decision of whether to provide rigorous instruction and then reteach the content to a significant proportion of the class or to reduce the quality of instruction and provide filler activities until students return. It is common for teachers to use filler activities during these times of year so that no students fall significantly behind.

   b. When parents are making decisions about whether to extend a vacation or take their student out of school in the days leading up to or after a break, they may ask their child, "Are you going to miss anything?" and the child responds, "We are just watching movies and playing games. I'll be fine." This exchange leads more parents to remove their child from school in the days surrounding a break.

   c. With fewer children in the class, the teacher continues to think that it is not worth providing meaningful instruction, and the cycle continues.

3. Have parents calculate the amount of learning time lost to this vicious cycle across a student's K–12 school experience. Ask the following questions:

   a. If this vicious cycle occurs in the week before and the week after winter break and spring break, how many weeks of reduced or lost learning time does this equal in the course of a single school year? (4 weeks)

   b. If this pattern continues across the 13 years of a student's K–12 school experience, how many weeks of reduced or lost learning time does this equal? (52 weeks)

4. Explain that 52 weeks of lost learning time is a year and a half of instruction, which means that a high school senior may graduate with only junior-year skills and abilities as compared with the skills and abilities of a senior in a school or district that does not have this problem.

(continued)

FIGURE 7.5 **(*continued*)**

---

5. Have parents discuss the following issue: Even if an individual family is willing and able to help their child catch up, the greater the number of individuals who decide to take their child out of school during these times, the greater the detrimental effect on all members of the classroom—the teacher, other students, and the absent student. Have parents brainstorm detrimental effects (e.g., the teacher has to prep significant makeup work for absent students; the teacher may not teach as rigorously—leading to less learning for all; students possibly graduating with fewer skills than peers at other schools).

6. Inform parents that teachers will be teaching every day leading up to a break and every day following the break. Encourage families to send their student to school every day that the student is not seriously ill.

Consider scheduling one or more high-value activities or motivational-system opportunities on the day just before the break and the first day back. We have heard stories of students begging their parents not to take them out of school early so that they can participate in these high-value opportunities. For example, one principal told us that a student's parents were going out of town in the week before the break, and the plan was for the student to stay with a grandparent in another city. When the school announced its plan for rigorous instruction in that final week, along with a series of fun schoolwide activities, the student begged his parents to allow him to stay with the other grandparent who lived in town, which allowed him to be in school every day.

If absences surrounding holiday breaks are particularly problematic in your school, see Chapter 8 for additional ways to provide universal strategies tailored to the specific reasons (e.g., taking time during the instructional school year to avoid busy times at major attractions or visiting families in other countries). Chapter 8 also provides suggestions for tailoring universal approaches when absences predictably increase at other times of year (e.g., fishing or hunting season or the first month of school).

Provide Strategies for Addressing Common Issues That Contribute to Absenteeism

Many parents would do more to support school efforts if the school made them more aware of specific problems and, even better, provided tools and strategies to support their involvement. Communicating with families to address widespread issues can help decrease the number of students who continue to experience attendance problems. Use the full range of methods available (e.g., parent training opportunities, letters home, social media, and newsletter articles) to communicate concerns about common issues and convey recommended strategies for supporting students and addressing those concerns. Consider the following possible approaches.

Provide tips on technology and social media use. Many problems that relate to absenteeism may originate from inadequately structured and supervised technology use at home. For example, when students stay up late with electronic devices in their bedrooms, they exhibit patterns of being too tired or ill to go to school. Or, when students are involved in cyberbullying or conflicts with peers online, they may increasingly avoid school. Many parents are unaware of the widespread drama or cyberbullying that occurs on social media and the negative effects that spill into the school environment. Even parents who are aware may not have the skills to help the child address the issue. Schools should provide parents with information on the frequency of problems their students are facing on social media and provide tips on the use of technology and social media. The handout shown in Figure 7.6 offers strategies for setting expectations and rules regarding technology use, teaching responsible digital citizenship, and providing supervision.

Educate families on "how sick is too sick?" Although illness is the leading reported cause of absenteeism, many excused absences for illness are for minor conditions that are not serious enough to warrant remaining home from school. Some excused absences for illness may also occur when a student is experiencing anxiety or simply wants to be with a family member or to do things that reinforce the desire to stay home, such as playing video games or watching movies. The student may express physical concerns (e.g., a headache or stomachache) to an adult caregiver when other symptoms are absent. A handout titled "How Sick Is Too Sick for School?" (see Figure 7.7) can help parents determine whether a child who is complaining of illness should stay home or go to school. When a parent answers "no" to each item on the checklist, the student is probably healthy enough to attend school. Have your school or district nursing staff review and adapt the checklist or develop one for your school. It may be beneficial to teach one or more lessons to students on how to use the checklist. Lessons should cover things like appropriate and inappropriate times to miss school. Redistribute this form and emphasize the contents with families and students at times of the year with increased illnesses (e.g., flu or allergy season).

FIGURE 7.6 **Handout for Parents on Dealing with Technology**

Technology: Tips and Strategies for Parents

In today's world, technology is everywhere. Children are exposed to technology in a multitude of forms throughout each day. They text, e-mail, use social media, surf the web, watch television and movies—the list goes on and on. In fact, for many children, technology is one of the main ways they interact with and learn about the world. Thus, it is important that they have some guidance as they negotiate this increasingly technological world.

We have created this tip sheet to help you consider what you can do to help your children remain safe, act responsibly with technology, and learn how to be good digital citizens.

Talk early and often with your children about safety when dealing with technology. Inform children that—

- They should never share passwords with anyone other than parents or guardians (even a best friend).
- They should never give out personally identifiable information.
- They should never give anyone their location or agree to meet in person with anyone they met online.

Discuss (in age-appropriate terms) identity theft, sexual and financial predators, and other risks, such as cyberbullying and privacy concerns.

Frequently discuss and review what appropriate and respectful behavior looks and sounds like when communicating through technology. Use the following guidelines:

- If you wouldn't do or say something in front of a trusted and respected adult, don't do it online or by text.
- Participating in cyberbullying by sharing, reposting, or commenting on negative remarks about someone else makes the problem worse. The only appropriate response is not to respond and to tell a parent or another adult about the cyberbullying immediately.
- If you wouldn't want a comment shared or said about you, don't share or say it about another person.
- Think before you post or text, especially if you are upset or angry. Once a photo or message is in the electronic world, it never goes away and can seriously affect your reputation, success, and future.
- NEVER send photos or images that contain nudity or messages with sexually explicit content.

Note: Sexting—sending sexually explicit photos or messages by phone or other technology—is a phenomenon that has become increasingly common, especially

FIGURE 7.6 **(continued)**

among teenage girls. It carries serious risks, such as messages being forwarded to others. In addition, those who send or possess sexually explicit photos of a minor can face felony child pornography charges.

Establish procedures and rules regarding technology in your household.

Set appropriate limits on how long and where technology can be used. Consider procedures and rules such as the following:

- Allow no more than two hours use of nonacademic technology each day on weekends, and less on weekdays.

- Some cell phones and computers can be set to have time limits or to prevent access during specified hours. Create a password for your child and set the device with the desired restrictions.

- Require that all electronic devices be turned off one hour before the child's bedtime. Studies have shown that bright lights (such as those from computers, cell phones, and TVs) can interrupt human sleep cycles and delay sleep.

- During dinner, place all cell phones (including parents' phones!) in a box away from the dinner table.

- Create the expectation that electronic devices are not allowed in children's bedrooms. This includes cell phones, computers, TVs, and gaming devices. One possible way to set this expectation is to establish a charging station in the parents' bedroom; all charging cords stay at this station. At bedtime, place all electronic devices in the parents' room to charge.

  Note: Technology should not be allowed in children's bedrooms for several reasons:

  o Electronic devices in bedrooms have been linked to sleep problems in children and teens. Lack of sleep contributes to attention problems, difficulty concentrating and learning, aggressive behavior, increased risk of depression, and a host of other health, behavioral, and emotional issues.

  o Access to technology in the privacy of the bedroom can lead to increased risk for sexting, cyberbullying and conflict, and engaging in behaviors that can put a child at risk for predatory behavior.

  o For children who have unsupervised access to technology, night is a prime time for cyberbullying. When a child is victimized through cyberbullying, it is important to limit and monitor the child's access to technology so that he or she is not bombarded with negative messages 24 hours a day.

(continued)

FIGURE 7.6 **(continued)**

- Create a Technology Contract that outlines specific rules and expectations for your children's use of technology. Include expectations for time, location, respectful and appropriate behavior, responsible use of personal information, appropriate and inappropriate sites, and how use will be monitored and supervised. You may wish to include "responsibility clauses" that allow children additional technology privileges for exceptional behavior as well as penalty clauses that outline potential consequences for violating aspects of the contract.

Supervise and teach your child about technology use.

Although filters and parental control features are available and can be a useful starting place, be aware that many children know how to bypass these controls. In addition, your child will likely visit places with no filters and no supervision. Therefore, the best supervisor and teacher is YOU!

Talk with your children about the websites they visit, what they do there, and who they communicate with.

When your children are first exploring technology, explore it with them and give guidance about good versus bad sites, how to evaluate the information they are viewing, and how to make responsible and safe decisions.

Periodically review your children's cell phone and computer histories. Set the expectation that only a designated adult can erase cell phone, browser, and e-mail histories. If the child erases a history, the adult should assume that something inappropriate has occurred and consequences should be put in place.

Over time, as your children demonstrate increased maturity, responsibility, and appropriate use of technology, you may decide to gradually release responsibility to them. However, always remain involved by talking with your children, providing periodic spot checks, and reminding them about the essentials of safety and responsibility as a digital citizen.

Additional Resources

Common Sense Media: commonsensemedia.org

Family Online Safety Institute: www.fosi.org

Internet Safety Tips for Parents, U.S. Department of Justice: www.justice.gov /usao/ian/psc/Elementary%20Safety%20Tips%20for%20Parents.pdf

FIGURE 7.6 **(*continued*)**

Kids and Technology: Tips for Parents in a High-Tech World, Centers for
   Disease Control and Prevention: www.cdc.gov/media/subtopic/matte
   /pdf/cdcelectronicregression.pdf

NetSmartz Workshop, National Center for Missing and Exploited Children:
   www.netsmartz.org/Parents

10 Ways to Keep Kids Safe Online, Tech Savvy: techsavvymag.com/2014/04/07
   /online-safety-kids-parents/

Tips for Parents, National Crime Prevention Council: http://archive.ncpc.org
   /topics/internet-safety/tips-for-parents.html

Source: From *Foundations Module E: Improving Safety, Managing Conflict, and Reducing Bullying,*
by R. Sprick, J. Sprick, and P. Rich, 2014, Eugene, OR: Pacific Northwest Publishing. Copyright © 2014
by Pacific Northwest Publishing. Adapted with permission.

Provide tips for improving students' sleep habits. Many students
miss school because they are not getting enough sleep and are overly tired, or
they get sick because their immune system is weakened. Figure 7.8 provides
an example of sleep tips that could be sent home to parents in a newsletter or
mail blast, or taught during a back-to-school or parent night. It may also be
useful to teach one or more lessons to students on how to get recommended
amounts of sleep and why doing so is beneficial. For example, one school
that used these tips for a lesson reported that teenagers in their school were
honestly unaware that consuming caffeinated beverages in the afternoon or
evening could disrupt their sleep patterns.

Share strategies to help students manage anxiety. Educators tell us
that many students are absent due to anxiety (either ongoing or temporary due
to a particular situation). These students stay home to avoid anxious thoughts
and feelings about matters such as academic performance, test taking, or peer
or adult relationships. They do not know techniques or have not figured out
how to regularly implement strategies for managing these feelings and associated symptoms. You can provide parents and students with the tips shown
in Figure 7.9. Review them with your school community during times when
increased anxiety is predictable (e.g., before and during high-stakes testing,
whenever a significant national or local crisis occurs, or when the school community or a class is experiencing significant upheaval or uncertainty).

FIGURE 7.7 **Handout for Parents: How Sick Is Too Sick for School?**

In general, children are too sick to come to school when—

- They are contagious.
- Their symptoms are serious enough to prevent them from focusing on the tasks they need to do in school.

Use this checklist to determine whether to keep your child home from school.

	YES	NO
1. Does your child have a fever of 100°F or higher?	☐	☐
2. Has your child vomited two or more times in a 24-hour period?	☐	☐
3. Does your child have diarrhea?	☐	☐
4. Are your child's eyes crusty, bright red, and/or discharging yellow or green fluid (conjunctivitis/pink eye)?	☐	☐
5. If your child complains of a sore throat, is it accompanied by fever, headache, stomachache, or swollen glands?	☐	☐
6. If your child complains of a stomachache, is it accompanied by fever, vomiting, diarrhea, lethargy, sharp pain, and/or hard belly?	☐	☐
7. Does your child have a persistent, phlegmy cough?	☐	☐
8. Does your child have lice (white, translucent eggs the size of a pinpoint on the hair or insects on the scalp)?	☐	☐

If you answered yes to any of these questions, please keep your child home from school and consider seeking medical attention. Your child could have a serious or contagious illness. Keep your child home until he or she has been symptom free for at least 24 hours or until the doctor indicates that he or she can return to school.

Children who have a cold, headache, or stomachache that is not accompanied by fever, vomiting, or diarrhea can probably come to school.

If your child has a rash, it could be contagious. Please seek medical advice before allowing your child to come to school.

Earaches are not contagious. Children can come to school if they can concentrate on their work.

Once your child has been treated for lice, he or she can return to school.

Source: From *Absenteeism and Truancy: Interventions and Universal Procedures*, by W. R. Jenson, R. Sprick, J. Sprick, H. Majszak, and L. Phosaly, 2013, Eugene, OR: Pacific Northwest Publishing. Copyright © 2013 by Pacific Northwest Publishing. Adapted with permission.

FIGURE 7.8 **Handout for Parents on Sleep Habits**

Tips for Improving Your Child's Sleep and Reducing Absenteeism

Did you know that your child (6 to 13 years old) needs 9 to 11 hours of sleep a night? Did you know that your teenager (14 to 17 years old) needs 8 to 10 hours of sleep each night? Inadequate sleep can lead to the following:

- Mood swings
- Behavioral problems
- Exacerbated symptoms of attention-deficit/hyperactivity disorder (ADHD) or misdiagnoses of ADHD
- Problems with learning
- Illness

Here are some tips to help your child get the sleep he or she needs.

- Minimize activities that involve bright lights, excitement, or stress in the hour before bedtime, including the following:
  - o Exercise
  - o Playing video games
  - o Using cell phones
  - o Watching television (Watching TV near bedtime has been associated with bedtime resistance, difficulty falling asleep, anxiety around sleep, and sleeping fewer hours.)
- Restrict cell phones and other electronic devices from your child's bedroom during sleeping hours. For example, have a charging station in your room where all electronic devices charge at night. (This is important for sleep as well as for reducing cyberbullying and other concerns that can come with unsupervised technology use.)
- Keep a regular and consistent sleep schedule and bedtime routine, even on weekends.
- Make your child's bedroom conducive to sleep—dark, cool, and quiet.
- Have your child avoid caffeine throughout the day and especially after midday.
- Have your child avoid large meals before bedtime.

Source: Based on information from the National Sleep Foundation and Centers for Disease Control.

FIGURE 7.9 **Handout for Parents on Anxiety**

Help Your Child Cope with Anxious Thoughts and Feelings: Relaxation and Anxiety Management Strategies

Most people experience anxiety or stress at one time or another. However, high levels of anxiety or stress can have negative effects, such as increased absenteeism, physical illness, and struggles in school. These tips can help your child manage anxiety and cope with stressful situations.

Note: If your child has significant and ongoing struggles with anxious thoughts and feelings, consider discussing this situation with your doctor, the school counselor, or another health professional to determine if additional supports are warranted.

1. Work with your child to identify and write down times and places that trigger anxious feelings. Also identify physiological changes that result from anxiety. Have the child reflect on times when he felt anxious, and identify if any of the following occurred: sweating, feeling shaky, increased heartbeat, or tension in certain parts of the body. If your child is unable to identify anxiety triggers or symptoms, it may be helpful for him to write in a journal whenever anxious feelings occur. Work together to look for a pattern across time.

   Encourage your child to use one or more of the relaxation techniques described below when in anxiety-producing situations and when experiencing identified physiological symptoms.

2. Teach and practice relaxation techniques with your child. Model and talk aloud as you initially demonstrate a technique. Then have your child practice with you. As your child demonstrates the ability to perform the technique with ease, encourage her to think about an anxiety-producing situation while practicing the technique. Find times each evening to practice one or more of the following with your child:

   • *Deep Breathing.* Have your child sit with a straight back or lie down. Have her breathe normally and notice how a normal breath feels. Demonstrate and then have your child practice breathing deeply, inhaling through the nose. Her abdomen should expand as she breathes deeply and fills her lungs. Her chest and shoulders should move only minimally. To exhale, your child should breathe slowly out through her mouth using an audible exhaling sound. Practice the technique while counting: 4 seconds to inhale, 7 seconds holding the breath, 8 seconds exhaling. Do at least 10 full-breath sequences during practice each day, and encourage additional sequences whenever your child is feeling anxious.

   • *Progressive Muscle Relaxation.* Have your child tense his toes (tightening the muscles as much as he can), hold for at least five seconds, and then release. Have him tense his calf muscles, tightening the muscles as much as he can,

FIGURE 7.9 (*continued*)

and then release. Have him work progressively through each major muscle group (i.e., thighs, buttocks, abdomen, arms and hands, neck and shoulder, jaw and lips, eyes). Direct your child to feel the difference between tension and relaxation. Discuss which muscles he might tense and relax when he feels anxious in the presence of others. The student could tense his toes, leg muscles, or hands without others knowing he is using the technique.

- *Visualization.* Have your child identify a place or situation she finds calming and ask her to describe as much as she can about the situation—sights, sounds, smells, physical sensations (e.g., heat, texture of the ground). Have your child sit and close her eyes. Initially practice by describing the place as she visualizes being in that place. Over time, switch to having your child visualize without any auditory cues.

3. Work with your child to maintain other healthy lifestyle choices that can help her feel her best:

- Drink plenty of water and limit caffeine.

- Get recommended amounts of exercise.

- Get adequate sleep for the age group. Children ages 6 through 13 need approximately 9 to 11 hours of sleep a night, and teenagers ages 14 through 17 need 8 to 10 hours of sleep each night.

- Do healthy things that your child enjoys and finds relaxing. Consider things like yoga, listening to music, volunteering, or talking to friends or family who have a positive and optimistic outlook and lifestyle.

- Get help for depression or anxiety as needed. Talk to someone at school or discuss ongoing concerns with a physician or therapist.

4. Seek out resources that may help your child, including the following:

Anxiety and Depression Association of America, "Tips to Manage Anxiety and Stress" (https://adaa.org/tips-manage-anxiety-and-stress)

Harvard Health Publishing, "Relaxation Techniques: Breath Control Helps Quell Errant Stress Response" (www.health.harvard.edu/mind-and -mood/relaxation-techniques-breath-control-helps-quell-errant -stress-response)

Mayo Clinic, "Relaxation Techniques: Try These Steps to Reduce Stress" (www.mayoclinic.org/healthylifestyle/stress-management/in-depth /relaxation-technique/art-20045368)

Provide recommendations for establishing a consistent bedtime and morning routine. Some students may struggle to get to school because they (and their parents) have difficulty keeping a consistent evening and morning routine. Every day may be a struggle to wake up on time, dress, gather all materials, and get in the car or on the bus on time. This situation leads to a chaotic and stressful start to each day as well as an increased likelihood of students and parents being tardy or absent. Provide tips to parents on how to establish routines, and consider how teaching all students these routines can help families and students establish healthy life skills. For students whose parents can't or won't participate in getting them ready for school, the tips in Figure 7.10 are essential so that the student can self-manage the routine despite family circumstances.

One of Jessica's students provides an extreme example of the kinds of challenges students may face in setting up and following routines. The student was frequently absent because he missed the bus in the morning and had no other transportation to school. As Jessica and her colleagues investigated the issue further, they found that the student was on his own to ensure he was up and ready for the bus, as his dad was sleeping when the student woke up for school. The student lacked habits for getting himself up on time and getting his things ready. They used the checklist approach with him, practicing necessary skills like setting his alarm at school and having a school-based adult mentor call him at home to walk him through the bedtime and morning routine at the outset of the plan. Although this approach worked in the short term, they also learned that the student lived in a tiny apartment and slept in a sleeping bag on his father's bedroom floor, as he had multiple older siblings who all shared another room. Part of what was making it so difficult for him to wake up and be ready for the bus was that his father stayed up until 2 or 3 a.m. each night playing video games in the bedroom, and the noise and light of the games kept the student awake. Although the checklist was helping get him to school each day, he was still exhausted and cranky throughout his classes because of lack of sleep. Jessica and her colleagues found a small tent for him and sewed dark fabric across the top so it would block out the light. They also purchased earplugs for him to wear to block out sound, and another staff member donated a camping mattress to cushion the floor where he slept. These things made a huge difference.

Although these steps were highly effective, they were time consuming for staff members; they worked on this elaborate plan after other, simpler interventions were attempted and proved unsuccessful. Obviously, schools do

FIGURE 7.10 **Handout for Parents on Establishing Bedtime and Morning Routines**

Take the Stress Out of Your Morning Routine

Tips for Establishing Effective Bedtime and Morning Habits

An hour before the bus will arrive, your child's alarm goes off. She hits the snooze button. The alarm goes off again. Snooze. You come in and tell your child to get out of bed. Ten minutes later she is still not up. You throw the covers off the bed and tell her to hop in the shower. After she showers, she takes 10 minutes to figure out what to wear. When she saunters down the stairs, she has 15 minutes to eat breakfast and get her things together. She turns on the TV and slowly eats her breakfast. With 3 minutes before the bus arrives, she runs around throwing things into her bag. As she runs out the door, you realize that she has left one of her textbooks behind. You run out the door after her.

If this scene or something similar plays out in your household, consider ways to establish consistent evening and morning routines. Have your child start getting ready for bed at least 30 minutes before the specified bedtime so that she gets everything ready for the next day and starts winding down for bed. Use a checklist before your child goes to bed each night so that you and your child won't need to scramble in the morning to get everything ready. After the routine is established, you may find that getting everything organized for the morning will also allow your student to sleep in a little later.

Before Bedtime

Tasks			Completed
1. **Pack school bag.**			☐
Homework?	yes	no	
Binder?	yes	no	
Pencil?	yes	no	
2. **Pack lunch and put in fridge.**			☐
3. **Set out clothes.**			☐
4. **Set alarm.**			☐
5. **Brush teeth.**			☐

(continued)

FIGURE 7.10 **(continued)**

Teach your child that the snooze button is not helpful, and consider taping over it or buying an alarm clock without a snooze function. Use a morning checklist to set a routine and ensure that your child reaches school with everything he needs.

In the Morning

Tasks	Completed
1. **Get up with alarm.** (No snooze!)	☐
2. **Shower (10 minutes max.) and get dressed.**	☐
3. **Brush teeth.**	☐
4. **Put lunch in bag.**	☐
5. **Take bag and wait for bus.**	☐

You may also wish to provide a reinforcing item or activity for your child when he uses the checklist and gets to school or the bus on time. For example, "After you use your bedtime and morning checklist and get to school on time for 10 days, I will take you and a friend to a basketball game." If a particular part of the routine is difficult for your child, consider reinforcing only that part. For example, if your child habitually hits *snooze* and you have to nag to get him up, reinforce when he does not use the snooze button. For example, "After five days of getting up without snooze or nagging, you get 30 minutes of extra TV time that night."

not have the time to do this kind of analysis, planning, and intervention with every student with attendance problems. Instead, you can use a multitiered approach to reduce the number of students who require individual interventions (intensive interventions of this sort are discussed more in Chapter 11). For example, if many students in your school struggle with a bedtime and morning routine, and if many parents lack appropriate habits for helping their child get adequate sleep, consider a schoolwide campaign to teach students and parents about the value of using bedtime and morning checklists, and to provide sleep tips and other relevant training for parents. Then provide increased instruction, support, and intervention for any children whose attendance does not improve after these schoolwide efforts.

Consider other problems that contribute to absenteeism in your school that might be addressed or alleviated by sharing tips and

strategies with parents. It may be beneficial to develop tip sheets and other information on topics such as these:

- How to identify, respond to, and report bullying and cyberbullying
- The importance of hand washing and other health tips (especially during cold and flu season)
- How to access supports available in the community for issues such as mental or physical health, addiction services, and homelessness
- How to help students with homework, organization, and social skills
- Self-advocacy skills and how to communicate concerns to the teachers and school

Many reputable sources have information available via the internet or in free brochures and pamphlets that can help you compile these tip sheets. For example, the U.S. government has a website (stopbullying.gov) that provides up-to-date information on topics such as "How to Prevent Bullying" and "Warning Signs for Bullying" that may be beneficial for parents. The Centers for Disease Control and Prevention (cdc.gov) has articles and tips for things like "Common Colds: Protect Yourself and Others" and "Protect Yourself from Wildfire Smoke" that might help prevent illness-related absences. You might also consult with local health care providers and district personnel to seek out relevant information and resources.

Celebrate Attendance Efforts and Successes with Families

Just as students and staff may be encouraged by acknowledgment and motivational systems as they work on improving attendance, parents may benefit from similar efforts. As the school makes progress toward its goals, ensure that communication with families acknowledges these improvements, even when they are small. Thank families for their collective efforts to build a culture of attendance. The following are examples of ways to do so.

Hold a celebration. Earlier in this chapter we mentioned the Big Bear BBQ that Barnes Elementary School in Kelso, Washington, holds as an end-of-year celebration to recognize the students who attended school for 95 percent or more of the year. All families and students are invited, along with local dignitaries and other prominent members of the community. The school serves barbecue food, and students play recess games. During the celebration, the school recognizes families of students with regular attendance using award certificates and raffle drawings.

Provide intermittent incentives for families whose students maintain regular attendance or demonstrate improved attendance. At various times of the year, randomly draw from the list of students with regular or improved attendance and provide a reward for their families. Consider school-based rewards such as lunch with the principal for a few families and students. Also connect with local businesses to see if any are willing to provide gift certificates, items, or coupons for goods and services. The following are examples of donations that our communities have enjoyed.

- $10 off a grocery bill at a local store
- Free drink coupon at a local coffee shop
- Free admission or "buy one, get one free" coupon to a local attraction or event, such as the zoo or a basketball game
- Free one-hour massage or facial

Have the principal or assistant principal make two brief phone calls each week to thank families of students who have regular attendance or who have made significant improvement in attendance. Most families expect that a call from the principal means their child is in trouble or there is some sort of emergency. A positive phone call from the principal is unexpected and can be highly meaningful, especially for students who struggle with school or are unlikely to be recognized in other ways.

Involve Community Stakeholders

It may seem farfetched to think that community involvement in an attendance initiative is likely or possible. However, we have seen that when schools make the case to community stakeholders, everyone steps up to support the efforts. Community members recognize that this issue can have a significant positive or negative effect on the community and on society. Community stakeholders can be involved in efforts to educate and motivate students and families, to help enforce and encourage students to be in school, and to volunteer to support students with attendance concerns.

Use Various Ways to Communicate and Engage the Community

To encourage participation from community stakeholders, share relevant information from Chapter 1 as well as any data you have collected about the prevalence of and negative effects from absenteeism in your school.

Determine the best way to communicate the vision that improving student attendance can improve student outcomes and reduce the likelihood of students dropping out and delinquent behavior in the community. Options for communicating with community members about the attendance initiative include the following:

- Holding community forums
- Having members of the attendance team, school staff, students, or parents speak at local business meetings, neighborhood meetings, and school board meetings
- Visiting, calling, and writing letters to businesses and organizations in your community

Partner with Community Leaders and Forums to Educate Students and Families and Provide Incentives

Contact prominent community leaders, businesses, and centers of activity for your families and students. Work with them to jointly educate students and families about the importance of regular attendance. Provide talking points, posters, and other information about the attendance initiative and ask for their help in communicating the vision of a schoolwide culture of attendance. For example, if school staff are active in religious organizations, ask them to communicate with leaders to see if they will speak to their congregation about the importance of regular attendance or post information in community meeting spaces. Also ask appropriate organizations if they are interested in donating goods, services, or coupons as incentives for students and families with regular and improved attendance. Here are some possible community leaders and organizations to enlist:

- After-school clubs and organizations (e.g., Boys and Girls Club, YMCA, 4-H)
- Coaches of kids and teen sports clubs and teams
- Relevant local government agencies (e.g., parks and recreation, transportation planning)
- Medical, dental, and mental health offices and service agencies
- Grocery and convenience stores, restaurants, arcades, and other businesses your students and families frequent

Randy once worked with the staff of the high school in a town that was a popular tourist destination—skiing in the winter, biking and hiking in the spring and summer. In an effort to improve school attendance and punctuality, the school staff devised one particularly notable strategy regarding a certificate declaring that the student "demonstrated dependability in attendance." The school also provided students with a certificate for punctuality and attendance based on having no tardies or unexcused absences during the semester and told the large local employers (including those resorts) to ask for those certificates when students applied for jobs. Predictably, employers gave preference to applicants who demonstrated that they would show up on time to their job every day based on their school record of attendance and punctuality. Over the course of the year, students learned to start an employment portfolio that included the attendance certificates. The following year, the school had seniors explain to first-year students that if they had regular attendance and punctuality, they could accumulate multiple certificates to share with employers by the time they might apply for a job.

Enlist Community Businesses and Agencies to Help Enforce and Encourage Attendance

Consider where students, who are supposed to be in school, go when they are not in school (e.g., convenience stores, arcades, restaurants, the mall). Communicate with the owners of these businesses and agencies to see if they are willing to encourage students to return to school when they are observed during school hours.

At a training session on addressing absenteeism, we were discussing the importance of community involvement, and participants shared the following two stories. They provide examples of how, after schools communicated concerns to local businesses, the business owners changed their practices and encouraged students to attend.

Convenience Store 1

The school determined that many students were becoming truant on their way to school. As students passed a convenience store near the school, they would go in and buy snacks, and then they would go to someone's house to play video games. When the school communicated the concern to the convenience store owner, he was so supportive of the school's efforts to increase attendance that he decided to close the convenience store for 30 minutes before school started so that he could encourage students to move on toward school.

Convenience Store 2

Another school identified a similar concern at a local convenience store. Although this store owner was not willing to close down for part of each day, he decided to play music that middle school students in his area generally disliked, both in the store and via outdoor speakers, so they would not want to stay in the area. He also agreed to encourage students to continue on to school.

Both participants expressed their surprise that these store owners were willing to go to these lengths to support the school's initiative to improve attendance. They also indicated that these efforts made a difference in students attending school regularly.

In addition to communicating with local businesses about ways to partner, coordinating these efforts with local law enforcement, local media, and students and families can go a long way toward developing a community focus on addressing specific issues that contribute to absenteeism.

Seek Volunteers Among Community and Family Members

Parts of your attendance initiative may require volunteer support. For things like a walking school bus to address transportation issues (see Chapter 8), mentoring interventions for students with resistant chronic absenteeism problems (see Chapter 10), or getting the word out to the community about the importance of regular attendance, consider how to enlist volunteers from the community and families in your school.

Consider creating an e-mail account that can be included on attendance posters and other messaging in the community so that anyone who is interested in volunteering or learning more about the attendance initiative can contact a school representative. As you communicate your vision for the attendance initiative, let the community know about opportunities for volunteering. Monitor the dedicated email account and follow up with everyone who makes contact. Be sure to follow all school and district protocols for background checks and volunteer safety procedures.

Lewisville High School in Lewisville, Texas, provides a powerful model of how working with school families and outside community volunteers can help address a school need. The staff at Lewisville High saw that their students needed more positive male role models, so they developed a volunteer program called "Grateful Dads." They sought volunteers to create a committee of men comprised of dads, uncles, grandfathers, and male neighbors. Each volunteer would come to school one or more Fridays a month to greet students at the doors of the school for the half hour before the first bell. The mission was to provide a simple and easy way to increase the number of active, visible, and positive male role models for their students. Although this program was not initiated to influence attendance, we can only imagine that for some students, the program increased their connectivity with the school and willingness to actively participate. We've heard that some students like the Grateful Dads so much that they circle back through the door so they can be greeted more than once. The volunteers love the program, too.

▨ ▨ ▨ ▨ ▨

Many educators feel helpless when it comes to addressing attendance issues because they view it as primarily a parent problem that they have limited power to change. Our work with schools has shown us that most parents simply have no idea how important regular attendance is for the success of their students, and that simple strategies can go a long way to change the behavior of many parents. In this chapter we have provided a range of strategies that you can use to increase parents' awareness and ability to ensure that their child is in school every day possible. We also have provided ideas for engaging members of the community, as we have been pleasantly surprised by how many community members will go to great lengths to contribute to the goal of better attendance for all students.

Strategies in the next chapter focus on how to tailor your attendance initiative to the specific causes of absenteeism that are relevant in your community. As you proceed through Chapter 8, consider how to engage families and the community in ways that will help you address these tailored universal priorities.

■ ■ ■ ■ ■

Summary of Tasks for Enhancing Family and Community Involvement

Use the following outline as a quick reminder of the tasks involved in enhancing your school's family and community involvement.

Launch the attendance campaign with families.

- Identify strategies the school will use with parents to generate understanding and enthusiasm for the attendance campaign.
- Determine when materials will be developed and by whom before launching the schoolwide campaign.

Provide ongoing communication about attendance efforts.

- Determine when and how you will regularly update parents about the following:
  - Their child's number of absences and attendance rate or category.
  - The whole school's attendance data (ADA and percentages of students in the Regular Attendance, At-Risk Attendance, and Chronic Absence categories).
- Determine how to increase communication with families during problematic times of the year.
  - Identify times of year when absenteeism rises and plan to increase communication during these times.
  - Develop a plan for increasing communication with families about attendance leading up to and immediately following major school breaks (e.g., winter break, spring break).
- Determine ways to increase parent awareness about common problems that contribute to absenteeism, and provide strategies to support parent involvement.
  - Identify common problems that contribute to absenteeism (review Chapter 3 for details on using data to identify common problems).
  - Determine what materials will be developed and by whom.

Celebrate attendance efforts and successes with families.

- Identify methods for communicating and acknowledging successes and improvements. Consider the following:
  - o Celebrations
  - o Incentives
  - o Acknowledgments

Involve community stakeholders in attendance efforts.

- Create a plan for sharing the rationale and school vision for regular attendance for all students.
- Identify businesses, community leaders, and other stakeholders who should know about the attendance campaign.
- Determine which community leaders, businesses, activity centers, and others should be enlisted for support with the following:
  - o Educating students and families
  - o Providing incentives to students and families
  - o Enforcing and encouraging attendance
  - o Volunteering to support students
- Determine who will communicate and coordinate with each stakeholder group, and when and how this will occur (e.g., by phone, in person, at a community meeting).
- Identify what information should be shared with each stakeholder group.

Implementing Tailored Strategies to Address Schoolwide Priorities

In previous chapters we described general approaches suitable for any student population. Although individual schools may select different individual strategies, the general procedures and implementation considerations remain largely the same. The approaches in this chapter are different because those adopted may vary widely by district and by school, depending on the specific causes of absenteeism. What may work to address absenteeism issues in a school in rural Wyoming is vastly different from what may work in urban Chicago or Los Angeles. Even within a district, schools may identify different causes of absenteeism and so require tailored approaches.

In this chapter we describe common causes of absenteeism. As you read, consider which ones may be affecting large numbers of your students. Review Chapter 3 (pp. 36–44) to determine data you should collect to identify the common causes of absenteeism in your school.

Some of these causes may seem outside the realm of what the school can influence. However, for each cause there are things that schools can do that have been demonstrated to make a positive difference in getting more students to attend regularly. This chapter concludes with examples of how schools can implement strategies tailored to address causes of absenteeism that affect large numbers of their students.

Understand Common Causes of Absenteeism

Causes of absenteeism can be broken down in many different ways. For the purposes of this book, we define five broad categories:

1. Lack of understanding about the importance of attendance
2. Barriers to attendance
3. Escape or avoidance
4. Desire to obtain or access something outside school
5. Lack of value placed on school

The following sections describe each cause in more detail and provide examples of possible causal subsets.

Lack of Understanding About the Importance of Attendance

Lack of understanding is perhaps the simplest cause to address, especially when a pattern of absenteeism is in the early stages (e.g., the student has just started formal school, or the student has just begun showing increased levels of absenteeism). This cause of absenteeism has two main subsets:

- Parents or students don't recognize the negative effects of absenteeism.
- The school does not place overt value on or emphasize the importance of attendance.

The strategies outlined in Chapters 1 through 7 will go a long way toward addressing this cause. If your school finds that this is a leading cause of student absenteeism, revisit the strategies in previous chapters and determine whether additional efforts are warranted.

Barriers to Attendance

Barriers are situations that prevent students from attending school. Even if students value school and want to attend, they encounter difficulties that make it a struggle or even impossible. Examples of common barriers include illness, dental problems, mental health issues, transportation problems, financial issues, and obligations other than school.

Illness. Illness is the number one reason that students miss school. However, many students who do not attend school because of illness have minor conditions that do not warrant staying home or have other reasons that are excused as illness (Kerr et al., 2011). Even with chronic conditions such as asthma, many absences can be prevented through combined school and family efforts. For example, in locations where there are significant outdoor pollution or allergy concerns, schools might create a protocol for checking pollutant or pollen levels prior to recess. On days when levels are risky for children and adults with respiratory problems, schools provide alternate indoor procedures for students with asthma or other respiratory problems. See page 152 for examples of how schools have addressed illness-related barriers to attendance.

Dental problems. Each year, students miss significant amounts of school for dental concerns such as cavities and gum disease. The National Institute of Dental and Craniofacial Research indicates that 59 percent of adolescents ages 12 through 19 have cavities in their permanent teeth and that 20 percent of students have untreated tooth decay (NIDCR, 2018). Students who live in poverty have less access to regular dental care than their peers and exhibit significantly higher rates of absenteeism due to dental problems (Pourat & Nicholson, 2009).

Mental health issues. Students with depression, anxiety disorders, or behavioral disorders such as attention-deficit/hyperactivity disorder are likely to have higher rates of absenteeism (Kearney, 2008). These students may have more difficulty coping with school stressors such as academic demands and relationships with peers and adults. In schools where students feel pressure to perform well on tests and achieve high GPAs, student anxiety is common and may cause some students to be absent. In schools where students experience significant life stressors related to poverty or trauma, or stressors at school such as bullying or a negative school climate, absenteeism may increase as students with ineffective coping skills avoid school or develop negative health symptoms.

Transportation problems. Transportation problems are wide ranging. In places where traffic safety or neighborhood violence is a concern, students may be absent from school when parents cannot transport them and feel it is unsafe for students to walk or bike. In other places, students may miss school when it is too hot or too cold outside and they need to wait for a bus or walk long distances to get to a bus stop or to school. See how some schools have addressed these kinds of transportation issues on pages 153–154.

Additional transportation concerns can occur when parents are unreliable with transportation (e.g., cannot afford gas or car repairs, have difficulty getting to work on time, have mental or physical health issues). Students who take the bus may face safety concerns on the bus or at the bus stop, or they may miss the bus and have no other way to get to school. One common concern we have heard from schools is that their districts or bus companies have a strict policy that a student can be bused to or from only one residence, so students who live in more than one home (e.g., lives in separate places with divorced parents, or stays with grandparents or other relatives) may be turned away from a bus operating on a route that is not the students' standard route.

Financial issues. As described in previous chapters, students whose families have financial issues are more likely to be chronically absent than their affluent peers. These students may have less access to health care, preventive medical treatment, and necessary medications. They are more likely to have difficulty with reliable transportation, unstable housing situations, or to be homeless. Students from low-income households may experience food insecurity—not having regular access to food—and may be absent because of related health issues, including anxiety or depression, or exhibit behavioral issues because of hunger. However, even something like inadequate access to clean clothes or wearing clothes that look overused or tattered can cause a student to avoid school. Some schools have addressed this issue by providing students with access to washers and dryers so that they always have clean clothes available.

Obligations outside school. We commonly hear from educators that students are absent from school to watch over ill or disabled relatives or to care for younger children. Some students may also remain home when a parent has mental health concerns or substance abuse issues because they are concerned that the parent will come to harm if left alone. Other students may have jobs that require them to work during school hours or cause them to lose sleep or be unable to manage demands like homework and test preparation, leading to increased absenteeism.

Escape or Avoidance

Many students who are absent may choose to stay out of school or complain of illness so that they can escape or avoid something in the school environment that they find aversive. The main causes of escape or avoidance behaviors are deficits in skills, particular people, and negative situations.

Deficits. Deficits in skills fall into three broad categories: academic, social, and coping. Each has its own issues to address.

Academic deficits. We cannot underestimate the potency of academic deficits for causing a student to avoid school. These deficits can include inability to read at grade level, gaps in mathematical knowledge, and difficulties with organizational skills. Because reading permeates all academic subjects and is the gateway for learning most skills in school, we encourage you to give special consideration to how reading difficulties may cause students to avoid school. The National Institutes of Health reports that "up to 10% of people have difficulty reading, including those of average and even above-average intelligence" (NIH, 2010). In many schools, the percentage is much higher. If schools do not provide adequate accommodation and remedial supports, consider the potential stress and frustration students with deficits in reading feel when they are continually given academic tasks that are beyond their capability. Academic deficits should be given careful consideration within your attendance initiative. The longer students exhibit patterns of excessive absence from school, the more likely they are to suffer academic deficits.

Social skills. Social skills allow people to communicate and relate to others. They include both verbal skills (e.g., expressing emotions or needs, negotiating) and nonverbal skills (e.g., active listening, body language, willingness to compromise). Students with deficits in social skills may avoid school because they lack positive relationships with peers and adults and find navigating the continuous social interactions of school difficult and aversive. Furthermore, students with these deficits are more likely to experience bullying situations, conflicts with peers and staff, and other situations that make school a difficult and stressful environment.

Coping skills. Coping skills are methods used to manage or overcome difficult and stressful situations. They include relaxation techniques for anxiety or frustration, and positive self-talk and self-advocacy skills that can be used when faced with difficult situations. When students lack coping skills, they may be unable to manage school stressors such as academic difficulties, bullying or conflict with peers, and transitions to new schools, classrooms, or activities. Some students who lack coping skills may find that home stressors are so significant that they cannot focus at school or make school a priority. Students with inadequate coping skills may also experience increased mental and physical health issues that prevent them from coming to school.

People. Students may stay away from school to avoid uncomfortable interactions with people, including conflict with peers or staff members or bullying situations. Students who lack conflict resolution skills may avoid school when they experience temporary or ongoing conflict with peers. A student may be unsure how to handle a fight with a friend or a breakup with a girlfriend or boyfriend, or may get into frequent arguments that make school an unpleasant and unfriendly experience. When students experience frequent conflict with staff, they may feel disconnected from school or unwelcome, leading to increased absenteeism. These students may also experience higher rates of suspension due to defiance or emotional escalation with peers or staff members.

When students are involved in bullying at school or with members of the school community, the school is likely to see patterns of increased absenteeism. For example, the national Youth Risk Behavior Survey indicated that 15.5 percent of students who experienced bullying reported that they missed one or more days of school in the 30 days before the survey due to safety concerns, in comparison with only 4.1 percent of students who missed school due to safety concerns but did not report experiences with bullying (Steiner & Raspberry, 2015). Students who are bystanders to frequent or highly disturbing acts of bullying may also be absent from school more often because they view school as a hostile environment or are made uncomfortable by bullying situations. Students who chronically bully others may experience suspension-related absences.

Situations. School climate is integrally related to students' attendance, and students in schools with positive climates have been found to have better attendance (American Psychological Association, n.d.). When a school is well managed and designed to foster positive adult and student relationships, when students are highly engaged in meaningful activities, and when students are challenged but experience high rates of success, they are more likely to want to attend school.

When any of the following conditions exist in the school environment, students may be less motivated to attend school or actively try to avoid school:

- Highly punitive and adversarial interactions occur between staff and students (e.g., staff members frequently use sarcasm or belittle students, staff members focus on negative behavior, students perceive that staff members are unfair or disproportionate in their attention to misbehavior).
- Classrooms or common areas are unsafe or chaotic.
- Students are frequently bored in class and lack engagement in relevant educational activities.

- Students experience embarrassment due to poorly designed or managed activities.
- The overall climate of the school is cold and uninviting.

Furthermore, if school staff struggle to build positive relationships with students, to respond effectively to misbehavior, or to structure environments for success, and if students have significant deficits in behavioral and social skills, high rates of out-of-school or in-school suspension may also contribute to chronic absenteeism. See pages 155–156 for examples of how schools might tackle climate issues and pages 156–157 for how to reduce exclusionary discipline practices.

Desire to Obtain or Access Something Outside School

Students may find something outside of the school environment more satisfying than being in school. They may seek peer or adult attention or access to tangible items and activities that are unavailable in school; they may find joy in school-sponsored activities that take them out of school (sports teams or clubs); or they may want to participate in seasonal activities.

Peer or adult attention. Students who are absent from school, especially those who are truant, may be spending time with peers who are also absent or who have dropped out. They find spending time with their peers far more enjoyable, especially if they struggle with academics or adult and peer relationships in school. Students who are members of gangs and miss school fall into this category.

Other students may be absent from school to gain adult attention. If parents work in the afternoon, night, or early morning, students may find that school hours are the only time they can gain a parent's attention. Students who have parents or other close family members deployed in a branch of the military or whose parents work or live in another state or city may be absent from school when these adults are visiting. Some students may miss school to gain the negative attention of school personnel or parents when they reprimand or provide punitive consequences for truancy.

Access to tangible items or activities. When students are absent from school, they often have access to highly reinforcing objects or activities, such as technology (e.g., television, video games, a computer), sleep, or food. Students may feign illness or ask to remain home with a minor cold or headache because they prefer to stay home watching movies or playing video games than go to school.

Some students may be unsupervised during excused absences, when truant, or when suspended. For some students, this unsupervised time allows them to engage in activities such as substance abuse, sexual activity, or illegal acts (e.g., graffiti or theft).

School-sponsored activities. Although absences for school activities are excused and are related to students' involvement in school, it is worth considering whether excessive school-activity absences may be causing a hardship for teachers as they seek to increase student learning. In some schools, students miss such significant amounts of school when they are involved in sports or clubs that teachers face difficulties deciding how to move instruction forward. One district shared with us that students who were involved in multiple school activities missed more than 40 days of school a year, and there were often times when classes were missing 25 percent or more of their students simply because of travel to competitions and other activity-related events. See examples of how districts can assess and address negative impacts of school-activity absences on pages 157–159.

Seasonal activities. Some school communities have predictable times of year when many students are absent for vacations or other activities like hunting, fishing, or travel. These activities often occur according to a regular schedule (e.g., the weeks before and after holidays or state or federally mandated hunting season), which allows for creative problem solving by adjusting the school calendar. Some communities, however, face challenges when these activities occur on an unpredictable schedule. For example, hunting caribou, whale, and other migratory animals may be an essential part of the local culture, but that migration does not occur at a set time each year. See how schools can address absences for seasonal activities on pages 154–155.

Lack of Value Placed on School

Student attendance may be affected when a particular parent, culture, or community does not see school as valuable. Absences may also occur when the school or community unintentionally sends messages that school is not for particular students or when a systemic societal message indicates that school does not serve certain students. This cause of absenteeism can be particularly difficult to address, but it is a common problem and needs to be addressed in a comprehensive and longitudinal way. See pages 159–161 for how one school has tackled this cause of absenteeism.

Identify and Design Plans to Address Common Causes of Absenteeism

Review the section in Chapter 3, "Periodically Analyze Additional Data to Determine Trends and Causes" (pp. 45–50), and determine how you will filter your data (by demographics, time of year) or gather additional data (via surveys, focus groups) to identify the common causes of absenteeism in your school.

Once you collect and analyze these data, choose one to three common causes of absenteeism to address within your attendance initiative. Over time you can gradually work on additional causes. Although the team will take the lead in identifying strategies to address each cause, consider conducting one or more brainstorming sessions with relevant stakeholders to identify possible universal prevention and early intervention strategies. These brainstorming sessions may include the team, staff members relevant to a particular cause (e.g., for health-related causes, include school and district nursing staff), the whole staff, students, parents, or community members.

After brainstorming, the team should select strategies that are most likely to succeed and are manageable and reasonable to implement. Determine when and how to involve relevant stakeholders. In some cases, you may decide to select strategies that can be implemented immediately and choose a longer timeline to work on resource-intensive strategies. For example, if the team identifies addressing asthma and respiratory infections as a major priority, the school might immediately begin monitoring pollen counts and outdoor air quality before sending students outside for recess and provide lessons to students and staff on avoiding scented lotions and body sprays. In the longer term, the team could work to have air ducts evaluated and cleaned and other environmental factors evaluated and addressed, conduct a fundraiser to purchase air purification units for each classroom, and create materials to send to families on reducing triggers for respiratory issues at home.

Use Tailored Strategies to Address Specific Causes of Absenteeism

Schools have found and implemented various strategies to address the specific causes of absenteeism that are common among their students. Here we present examples of strategies that might be beneficial to address specific causes of absenteeism.

Implement Strategies to Address Asthma

The CDC (2014) reports that over 6 million children (under the age of 18) have asthma. Asthma is more common for students who are living near or below the poverty level than for students from higher-income households.

Schools working to address high rates of asthma and related absences have reported using strategies such as the following:

- Determine how to reduce pollutants at school (e.g., inspect air ducts, examine cleaning supplies to assess levels of toxicity, work with district to replace portable facilities that have poor ventilation or mold issues).

- Monitor air pollution levels and provide alternate indoor activities for the whole school or for affected individuals whenever there are high levels of pollution due to fires, factory activity, or stagnant weather patterns.

- Work with families and community agencies to identify and reduce common triggers for respiratory infections at home, such as tobacco smoke, dust mites, and mold.

- Partner with the school community to provide air purifiers and humidifiers in classrooms and to families of students with asthma.

- Provide evidence-based information to staff and families on how to help students manage and control asthma, as well as how to respond during an asthma attack. See www.cdc.gov and speak with healthcare providers and nursing staff in your district for resources.

- Institute policies to reduce air pollution, such as these:
  - Prohibit student and staff use of scented lotions, body sprays, and perfumes.
  - Create a clean-air policy that asks parents not to leave cars idling when picking up or dropping off students.

- Work with community agencies and families to ensure that students who have symptoms of asthma or respiratory illnesses are identified and linked with proper care (e.g., access to adequate health insurance, receive flu and pneumococcal vaccines, access and ability to use medications).

- Have school or district nursing staff conduct home visits for students and work collaboratively with families to identify and address asthma triggers.

Reduce the Impact of Medical and Dental Appointments

One group of schools we worked with identified medical and dental appointments as one of their main causes of absenteeism. They determined that families often scheduled appointments at the same time of day, which created an adverse impact on particular subjects. Students also remained out of school far longer than needed for the appointment (e.g., they went out to lunch or remained absent for the remainder of the day) and were sometimes absent when a sibling or parent had an appointment and transportation was difficult. The district implemented strategies such as the following and reported significant gains in attendance:

- Work to reduce preventable illnesses and dental issues that might require appointments (e.g., increase hand-washing initiatives, encourage and facilitate vaccinations, teach lessons on dental care).

- Communicate with local medical and dental offices about the importance of school attendance and ask them to post relevant information in their offices.

- Request that parents attempt to schedule appointments outside school hours and ask medical and dental offices to offer appointments before or after school before suggesting times during school hours.

- Teach parents and medical and dental providers to review a child's appointment history when scheduling appointments to see if times can be varied. For example, if the child had an appointment in the morning, try to schedule the next appointment in the afternoon.

- Clarify policies and teach students and families that the student must attend school before an appointment and return immediately after the appointment (e.g., the student should be absent only for the time spent going to, at, and returning from an appointment).

- Work with families to identify alternative transportation options when a parent or sibling has an appointment (e.g., arrange carpools, encourage busing options).

Troubleshoot Transportation Concerns for Students with Long Walks

Schools often have a one- to two-mile radius around the school that defines a zone where students do not have access to a bus and are expected to walk, bike, or be driven to school. When they break down absenteeism by neighborhood of residence, many schools find that the students who live on the outer edges of this "no busing" zone are absent more frequently than others. Some districts have also found that the farther students are from a bus stop, the more they tend to be absent. These trends are even more pronounced in places where the weather gets very cold or hot, or where there are significant concerns about neighborhood violence, unsafe traffic crossings, or bullying on the way to school. When schools identify these trends, they might explore combinations of the following options:

- In states where school funding is related to attendance, break down the potential cost of days lost to transportation problems and consider adding additional buses or bus stops for students who have to walk long distances.
- Coordinate a school carpool and ensure that students with the longest walks are personally invited to join the carpool.
- Arrange a *walking school bus* that uses routes of volunteers who can walk and escort students who live in the no-busing area. Walking school buses can help address dangerous traffic crossings and bullying problems on the route, and also create increased accountability for attendance among students who are frequently absent.
- Arrange clothing drives for jackets, boots, hats, gloves, and other items, and seek donations from families, community members, and businesses. Ensure that students and families know how to access these clothing resources. If there is concern that students will feel embarrassed, consider holding an evening clothing swap where families can bring lightly used clothing and swap for other items. If families do not have the resources to swap, encourage them to come and get what they need.

Address Absences Related to Vacations or Seasonal Activity

Many schools see a spike in absenteeism during specific times of the year due to family activities and travel. In some parts of the United States, fishing and hunting seasons lead to predictable increases in student absences. For any of these situations, consider one or more of the following solutions:

- Teach additional lessons to students and families about the importance of attendance before and during these times of year. Review the sample lesson in Figure 7.5 on page 121 about the effects of extending vacation into instructional time.

- Ensure that teachers continue to provide rigorous instruction during these times so students and families cannot claim that students who are absent won't miss anything important.
- Alter the school calendar to accommodate families who must travel for an extended period around winter break.
- Provide a fall break or hunting holiday in communities where hunting or fishing is an important and common family activity.
- Work with scientists to identify migratory patterns of animals that are hunted in the community so that breaks can be scheduled when animals are predicted to be in the area.

The more a particular cause is prominent for large numbers of families, the more the attendance team and school should do to consider a wide range of options. For example, if only three or four families are absent to visit family members around winter vacation, changing the school calendar is probably not warranted. However, if 50 percent of your families travel during this time and asking them to shorten visits with family would cause hardship, it is reasonable to consider something as extensive as an alteration in the schedule.

Design Plans to Resolve School Climate and Safety Issues

Concerns about school climate and safety can contribute to absenteeism for a large part of a school's population. If students have frequent behavior problems and rates of suspension are high, the school will need to design a comprehensive plan to address the problems. Efforts to improve school climate should be led by a site-based team such as a Positive Behavioral Interventions and Support (PBIS) team or a Multitiered System of Support for Behavior (MTSS-B) team. The first step for the team is to identify climate concerns using multiple ways to gather data, such as the following:

- Provide an anonymous climate and safety survey to assess areas of strength and weakness in the school. When possible, survey staff, students, and parents to get a sense of how each group views issues such as the prevalence of bullying, how safe students feel in different parts of the school, and levels of respect between different groups (e.g., staff to students, students to staff, students to students, staff to staff).
- Observe common areas and classrooms to identify locations and behaviors that might require additional training for staff related to

providing active supervision, interacting positively with students, and offering effective corrective feedback.

- Review behavioral data such as office disciplinary referrals, absenteeism, and truancy records for particular times or locations (certain classrooms, gym) where there may be unaddressed problems. Conduct observations in areas of concern.

- Conduct focus groups with students, parents, and staff to identify concerns about climate and safety.

Based on reviews of multiple data sources, identify one or more priorities for improvement, such as these:

- Increasing academic engagement and motivation and reducing boredom in classes

- Ensuring physical and emotional safety of students and staff (e.g., reducing fighting, eliminating threatening and bullying behavior)

- Creating caring and supportive relationships between staff and students

- Improving staff supervisory skills (e.g., active supervision, increasing positive interactions, providing effective corrective feedback)

- Creating a full continuum of multitiered problem-solving processes for both academic and behavioral support that allow you to identify and intervene with students at universal, targeted, and individualized levels

More than 30 years of research on behavior management shows that PBIS is an effective approach for improving the safety and positive climate of schools (Carr et al., 2002; Jenson, Rhode, Evans, & Morgan, 2013; Sprick, Garrison, & Howard, 2002; Sugai & Horner, 2006). If your school already has effective school improvement procedures for working on climate priorities, use them to address the selected priorities. If your school does not have a framework for implementing positive behavioral supports or would like additional support, these organizations are leaders in providing evidence-based practices for positive behavior support: Safe & Civil Schools (www.safeandcivilschools.com), Technical Assistance Center on PBIS (www.pbis.org), and Project ACHIEVE (www.projectachieve.info).

Reduce the Frequency of Out-of-School Suspension

If your school has high rates of out-of-school suspension (OSS), try to reduce the behaviors that lead to suspensions and concurrently create a range of strategies for correcting misbehavior to avoid overusing OSS. In addition to adding to a student's absences, OSS is associated with the following effects:

- Increased involvement with the judicial system
- Lower academic achievement
- Dropping out of school
- Higher rates of grade retention

Although these drawbacks are well known, OSS is used frequently for offenses that are not zero-tolerance. (Zero-tolerance offenses are often related to weapons and drugs.) According to the Civil Rights Data Collection, millions of children are suspended out of school each year—3.45 million public school students in 2011–2012, for example—and these suspensions are disproportionately assigned to students from minority groups.

Being suspended can set up an increased probability of truancy or subsequent suspension. Most families cannot take days off work to supervise the student during the suspension. Unsupervised, students can do whatever they want, and there is a big risk that they will find that being out of school brings less pressure and is more fun than being in school, setting up a high probability of a vicious cycle—the more school missed, the harder school becomes, and so not going to school becomes more attractive.

Administrators have the discretion to use other corrective consequences for the vast majority of offenses—consequences that can keep the student in school and continuing to learn. Plan to explain to staff that administrators' efforts to use consequences other than OSS are intended to support teachers by not rewarding the student with a three- or five-day vacation.

To reduce the behaviors that lead to office referrals, train staff to use consequences other than office referral. At the same time, it's important to remind yourself and other administrators to use an array of alternatives to OSS. See the recommendations in the previous section ("Design Plans to Resolve School Climate and Safety Issues"), because the same approaches can help address the problem of overusing OSS.

Assess the Impact of Absences Related to School-Sponsored Activities

Absences for school activities like sports and clubs can be particularly difficult to address because some stakeholders feel so strongly about school activities that it can be difficult to hold a discussion about reducing related absences. However, when schools suspect that school-activity absences are contributing to the negative effects of absenteeism, it is worth a deeper look to determine if starting discussions with the school community is warranted. Assess the frequency and negative effects of school-excused absences for activities through the following means:

- Conduct a survey of teachers to identify their level of concern about school-activity absences and determine whether these absences are causing a hardship for them and their classes.
- Look at attendance data to determine frequency of absences:
  - Identify the total number of school-activity absences across the student body, the average number of absences for involved students, and the number of absences accrued for students who participate in multiple sports and activities across the year (e.g., "One student participates in debate team, band, soccer, track, and baseball, and he had 22 school-activity absences last year").
  - Identify the attendance category for students who are involved in these activities (e.g., "Thirty-two students who have school-activity absences are in the Chronic Absence category").
  - Identify how schoolwide attendance percentages change when school-activity absences are not included as compared with when they are added in (e.g., "When we don't include school-activity absences, 9 percent of students are in the Chronic Absence category, and when we include school-activity absences, 15 percent of students are in the Chronic Absence category").
- Look at GPAs and test scores of students with frequent school-activity absences to see if some students may be falling behind because of these absences.

If any of these data sources indicate that school-activity absences are having a negative effect, consider the following options:

- Hold forums with the school community to discuss concerns about these absences and work with families to identify possible solutions.
- Work with coaches, leagues, and other entities to see if school-based or team-based accommodations could minimize absences or the negative effects of absences.
- Tighten policies so that students who are involved in sports and clubs will not be excused unless they maintain high levels of academic and behavioral success (e.g., As and Bs, no behavioral referrals).

- Design policies stating that absences for school activities may not be excused when students are frequently absent for other reasons.

- Encourage families to consider the number of activities their children are involved in during the year and whether they are missing too much school. In some cases, staff may need to meet with families to help make decisions about specific activities that require school absences.

- If activities typically occur during certain days and times, consider schedule alterations for individual students or the whole school. For example, if games are always on Friday afternoons, the school might schedule early release on Friday afternoon so that staff meetings occur when students are frequently absent. Or the school might schedule all students who participate in these sports in a PE class during the last period of the day so that absences have minimal effects on academic activities and the students are effectively conducting their PE activities through participation in the sport.

Understand and Address Cultural Barriers to Attendance

In some communities, a disconnect between the school and the community serves as a barrier to attendance and other school goals. Parents and the community at large may have had negative school experiences or feel that the school system did not serve them well. They may view the school system with skepticism or hostility that makes school improvement efforts difficult. The education system may even be viewed more as a threat than a positive force—the more students are educated, the more likely they are to reject certain cultural values of the community or leave the community to pursue further education and job opportunities. If these conditions apply to your community, messages that emphasize the importance of attendance (as described in previous chapters) are less likely to be effective at the outset and may actually create additional distance between school staff and family members. The following anecdote provides an example of how one school improved attendance by listening to and addressing the needs and values of the community.

Shungnak is a village in the Northwest Arctic Borough of Alaska in which the student population of the village and school is more than 90 percent Alaska natives. We began working with them to improve school climate and safety and to reduce out-of-school suspensions. Early on, the staff realized that one of the greatest barriers to a positive and productive school climate was family disengagement. Part of the problem was that the majority of the teaching and administrative staff was from the lower 48 states of the United States, and the community members felt that the school personnel did not understand, respect, or represent their cultural values.

To understand and begin to address these concerns, staff visited homes and listened to parents express their concerns about the school system, struggles they faced, and what they wanted from the school. Principal Roger Franklin indicated that many community members simply wanted to know how the school was going to help their community, and so the school staff worked with the community to identify how the school could become more integrated into community life. Principal Franklin said, "Our expectation [as a school] was to get parents to fully understand 'we are a family'—the village, school, and everyone that lives in Shungnak. That we are all responsible and accountable for one another."

As schools in the district, including Shungnak, made great progress with their climate and safety initiative, the relationship with the local community began to change, and school attendance was identified as a major priority by the school staff. The staff at Shungnak decided that their attendance initiative needed to start with parents. They wanted to increase parent presence in the school to ensure greater partnerships and relationships and designed a Parent Attendance initiative. They placed a wall chart in the office with a card for each student, similar to a time-punch card. Each family designated an adult representative who would go to the school for five minutes each week. When the five-minute (or longer) presence was completed, the family member could punch their student's time card and move it into the wall chart (see Figure 8.1). The goal was to have at least 90 percent of families attend school for five or more minutes each week, visiting classrooms, eating lunch with students, or simply greeting students in the hallway.

To roll out the initiative, the staff provided information using different media and opportunities, including announcements on VHF radio, at culture and skill-building workshops, and at local sporting and cultural events. They used word of mouth at the post office, airport, local stores, and during fishing and hunting excursions.

In the first two years of Shungnak's Parent Attendance initiative, student attendance improved from 68 percent to 89 percent ADA. The staff reports that parents and other family members have begun to stay longer at the school and volunteer, and parents have started taking pride in and responsi-

FIGURE 8.1 **Wall Chart for Parent-Attendance Initiative**

Source: Shungnak Elementary School, Shungnak, Alaska. Copyright © 2018 Shungnak Elementary School. Used with permission.

bility for seeing their children excel in school. Parent presence has enhanced the positive climate of the school, and the relationship between the school and the community has drastically changed.

▪ ▪ ▪ ▪ ▪

Causes of absenteeism differ greatly from community to community, and even between schools within the same community. Therefore, you should tailor the universal procedures in your schoolwide attendance plan to address the specific factors that contribute to absenteeism for large numbers of your students. Chapter 9 provides a universal Tier 1 focus as it describes how to analyze and revise your attendance policies over time to address the attendance patterns of your students. As you read Chapter 9, consider whether policy changes would help address any of the common causes of absenteeism in your school.

■ ■ ■ ■ ■

Summary of Tasks Related to Implementing Tailored Strategies to Address Schoolwide Priorities

Use the following summary as a quick reminder of the tasks involved in implementing tailored strategies that address your schoolwide priorities.

Understand common causes of absenteeism.

- Determine who should receive information on causes of absenteeism and how the information is best disseminated (e.g., a memo or a presentation).
- Develop preliminary hypotheses about causes of absenteeism that may be affecting large numbers of students in your school.

Identify and design plans to address your school's causes of absenteeism.

- Indicate how and when you will collect data to determine causes of absenteeism in your school.
- Identify one to three common causes of absenteeism that will be the focus of your attendance initiative.
- Conduct brainstorming sessions for possible strategies to address each of the identified priorities.
- Identify strategies that are most likely to succeed and are manageable and reasonable to implement.
- Determine who will be responsible for carrying out tasks and when tasks should be completed.

Implement tailored strategies to address each of the common causes.

- Monitor attendance and other related data across time to evaluate priorities and make adjustments as needed.

Analyzing and Revising Attendance Policies

As your school continues to build a culture of attendance through strategies discussed in Chapters 1 through 8, begin to analyze school and district policies to determine if they are aligned with your attendance initiative. Attendance polices often reflect a traditional approach, which is highly reactive and punitive, focusing solely on the metric of truancy (unexcused absence). Consider how you can revise attendance policies to reflect the school's goal of regular attendance for all students and to provide relevant information to families and students on how your school will monitor and address attendance concerns. In addition, recognize that attendance challenges are not static; new student populations and unforeseen changes might alter overall attendance rates, requiring school leadership and staff to be flexible. Every year, reflect on whether policies are appropriately designed to bolster your attendance initiative and help prevent the majority of attendance problems from occurring. Districts should conduct a formal analysis of policies every three to five years, using a team of representatives of key stakeholders (e.g., district administrators, building administrators, teachers, interventionists, and family and community partners).

In this chapter we suggest how you can revise existing policies to maximize attendance across your school. As a team, work through this chapter and analyze your existing policies, noting possible areas for change. The more prevalent a problem is within your school, the more you should consider how policies can be written with enough specificity and clarity to address it. For example, if excessive excused absences for illnesses are a significant problem, consider how your policy can clarify what is truly an excusable illness and specify measures that will be taken if a student exhibits a pattern of excused absences for illnesses that may not be legitimate.

Follow standard school and district procedures for assessing policy recommendations and making changes based on board approval or other required procedures. As policy changes are being reviewed and approved, create a plan for how any new policies will be taught to and reviewed with staff, students, and families. Also plan how to update any relevant documents (e.g., student handbook, school website, staff handbook) to reflect policy changes.

Refer to State Laws and District Policies

Ensure that your policy complies with any state laws and district policies that relate to student attendance. All states have compulsory attendance laws and most include legal procedures for dealing with habitual truancy. These laws and procedures should be explicitly described in your policy.

Some districts have clearly outlined policies that indicate measures the district puts in place at successive stages of intervention. Typically, these policies provide information related to punitive procedures such as truancy court, but districts may be moving toward defining policies related to chronic absenteeism. Ensure that relevant district procedures are defined in writing in your school policies.

Refer to Important Attendance Metrics

If state and district policies do not include metrics for Regular Attendance, At-Risk Attendance, Chronic Absence, and Severe Chronic Absence, update policies to include information on the goal of attaining Regular Attendance and avoiding At-Risk Attendance, Chronic Absence, and Severe Chronic Absence. Policies should clearly highlight that all students should have regular attendance (absent 5 percent or less), and that the school will intervene when problematic patterns of absence are identified (e.g., if the student is in the At-Risk Attendance, Chronic Absence, or Severe Chronic Absence category).

The metrics are calculated as follows using a combination of unexcused absences, excused absences, and suspension:

- Regular Attendance: Absent 5 percent or less of the school year
- At-Risk Attendance: Absent 5.1 percent to 9.9 percent of the school year
- Chronic Absence: Absent 10 percent or more of the school year
- Severe Chronic Absence: Absent 20 percent or more of the school year

Clarify the Definition of Excused Absence

Indicate appropriate reasons for excused absence, such as the following:

- Illness
- Funeral or death of a family member
- Medical or dental appointment
- Religious holiday
- Required court appearance
- School-sponsored curricular or extracurricular activity
- Other emergency

Provide specificity and clarity about each reason, as appropriate. The more often a particular reason for absence is occurring within your school and leading to adverse effects for students, the more closely the policy should be evaluated and revised. The following sections give examples of how to provide greater specificity and clarity for each reason for absence.

Illness

Specify that illnesses are excused only when they are "severe injury or illness too severe for the student to attend class." This specificity can help prevent parents from excusing minor illnesses, physical complaints, or things like sleeping in. Include the form titled "How Sick Is Too Sick for School?" (see Figure 7.7, p. 128) in the policy or as a supplementary document, and indicate that if a student is frequently absent because of illness, the student may be flagged to receive follow-up phone calls. A counselor, nurse, or principal will ask the parent the questions on the form. If a student continues to have illness-based absences but has no record of a chronic illness or other record from a physician, the school may initiate follow-up procedures such as requiring a doctor's note to excuse an absence or having the school nurse evaluate the child before an absence is marked as excused.

Consider what should be included in policies to address what will be done when a student has a chronic illness, contagious disease, or other illness documented by a physician that requires frequent absences from school. Options for continuing education when a student cannot be in school may include online courses or tutors, robotic or video-conference presence in classes, and face-to-face tutoring in the home setting. Although it is beyond the scope of this discussion to provide specific recommendations, you will need to consider school and family resources along with policies and procedures regarding legitimate extended absences. To whatever extent possible, the school leadership needs to ensure that the school is doing everything possible to help the student succeed.

Funeral or Death of a Family Member

Within your school's guidelines, it may be appropriate to offer some clarification on the relationships for which student absences are expected and not expected. It may be appropriate to identify which family members are usually covered by this reason for absence (e.g., nuclear family, grandparents) and to note that absences are not typically excused for a distant relative who has little personal relationship with the student (e.g., second cousin twice removed whom the student has never met). However, be sensitive to cultural issues. For example, in close communities such as those in native Alaskan villages, attending funerals for distant relatives may be an essential cultural value, so you may wish to include a statement that is more flexible, such as this: "For extended family members or the death or funeral of a nonrelative, please discuss with the principal." Also clarify how many days of absence will be excused and that special circumstances (e.g., extended travel or time) require discussion with an administrator.

Medical or Dental Appointments

Require a note from a doctor or dentist to excuse medical or dental appointments. Note that appointments should be scheduled outside school hours whenever possible and that appointment times should be varied as much as possible when they occur during school hours (e.g., morning, then afternoon). Specify that the student will be excused only for the time spent at the appointment and going to and from the appointment. If an additional procedure is needed to ensure that students do not extend the appointment time to go out to lunch or run other errands, for example, consider requiring that the note from the doctor's office specify the time the student entered and exited the office. Indicate that the student will be counted as excused only for transit time and time spent in the office. Depending on the severity of this problem, this procedure can be implemented in your policy as a whole-school measure or as a follow-up measure when a student is identified as having this particular attendance problem.

Religious Holiday

Specify that the religious holiday must be part of the student's religion or that permission must be obtained from the administrator. Include a list of approved holidays. Many states specify which religious and other holidays are approved, and this information can be obtained by contacting your state department of education or looking on their website. If this information is not available, or if you have students from religions that are not common in the area and are not included in state recommendations, consider working with religious leaders from each major religion represented in your school or district to identify holidays of particular significance. Indicate that any holiday not on the list requires permission from an administrator before it is considered as a reason for an excused absence.

Required Court Appearance

Indicate that the student will be excused only for the time spent in court and the time going to and from the court appearance. Specify the documentation needed to verify the court appearance.

School-Sponsored Curricular or Extracurricular Activity

Indicate that the student will be excused only for the time spent going to the activity, during the activity, and returning from the activity. Specify the documentation needed to verify the student's attendance at the activity. Also clarify requirements about minimum grades, classwork and homework makeup policies, and other expectations students must maintain in order to participate in school activities. For example, students must demonstrate that they have turned in all required work or have been granted an extension to be excused for a school-sponsored activity, or students must maintain a *B–* or better grade in all their classes. Work with your school community and district to determine appropriate thresholds for participation.

Other Emergency

Indicate that absences in this category will be excused only with administrator approval and provide examples of reasons that would qualify as "other emergency." Refer to unapproved reasons for absence (see descriptions in the next section) to clarify absences that are not considered an emergency.

Clarify Which Situations Will Not Be Excused

Make it clear that the school will not record absences as excused even if parents call for reasons such as the following:

- Vacations
- Minor illnesses (cold, stomachache, or headache when not accompanied by fever over 100 degrees, vomiting, or diarrhea)
- Haircuts
- Birthdays
- Taking a driver's test (unless the DMV is closed outside school hours)
- Shopping
- Car trouble (student or parent)
- Oversleeping (student or parent)

The more you anticipate resistance from families or students or a lack of understanding about why absences will not be excused, the more detailed the rationale in the policy should be. For example, if many families take extended vacations and expect these absences to be marked excused if they call in, provide a rationale such as this:

> Because attendance is critical for student success and an effective school community, vacations will not be considered excused even if a parent provides permission. Extended travel experiences should be scheduled during winter break, spring break, or summer vacation. When this is not possible, absences will be marked as unexcused. If a student has no or few other absences during the school year, unexcused travel absences may not result in further action from the school. However, if the student accumulates additional absences for other reasons, has 10 percent or more days missed across the school year or term to date, and/or has difficulty maintaining adequate academic or behav-

ioral success, referral for Tier 2 or 3 intervention and/or truancy court procedures may be initiated.

Define Times for Tardy and Absent Designations

Determine how long a student must be absent in order for the time to qualify as an absence rather than a tardy. For example, in some schools, a student is considered absent when gone for more than 10 minutes, in others it is 30 minutes, and in others it is only if the student is absent for the full day. In general, we do not recommend counting only full-day absences because partial-day absences that occur repeatedly at the same time of day (e.g., missing the first hour of school every day) will have a significant adverse effect on that time period. If the official record counts only full-day absences, ensure that you define informal ways for teachers and other staff to monitor and request assistance when particular students develop a pattern of partial-day absences.

Clarify When Attendance Will Be Taken Each Day

Specify how often attendance will be taken and ensure that staff members take responsibility for recording attendance at specified times. In elementary schools, we recommend taking attendance at least every morning, midday, and in the last hour of the afternoon so that students with partial-day absences are identified. It is common for elementary schools to have many students absent during the first or last hour of school. Taking attendance at these times as well as midday enables you to compare data for the three times to see if specific efforts are needed to address morning or afternoon absences. In secondary schools, it is critical to take attendance every period, as students often become truant only during certain periods of the day. We recommend analyzing data period by period to identify if there are times that are particularly problematic, and to see if some students have chronic absence during individual periods even if their overall attendance record indicates something different.

A personal experience of Randy's illustrates the value of taking attendance each period in secondary school. The high school he attended took formal attendance only for first period and then produced an attendance list that subsequent teachers could use for their own rosters rather than retaking attendance each period. Most teachers did not keep class-by-class attendance records. When Randy was a senior, he arranged to have first period study hall. His parents wrote a note to the school stating that he had an evening job and that he would use the extra time in the morning to sleep. Because his grades were pretty good, the school allowed this, which meant that he was never on the school's absentee roster. In the second semester, he had one teacher who took attendance later in the day. By the end of the semester, that teacher's records indicated that Randy had started skipping so frequently that he had missed 40 days of class! When the teacher asked about the situation, Randy claimed that as senior class president, he had work that needed to be done related to that role. Because he was able to keep his grades up, no one called him on this scam. The moral of this story is to review your school's policies to ensure that every class takes attendance and records are accurate, and to look for holes in the system—because if there are holes, even fairly responsible students may game the system.

Define Policies Related to Makeup Work/Course Credits/Grade Reductions Due to Absenteeism

Define policies related to makeup classwork and homework for excused absences versus unexcused absences or suspension. Because we do not know of concrete research on whether or not there should be penalties (e.g., reduction of points) for work that occurs during unexcused absences or suspensions, or what those penalties should be, we recommend getting input from teachers about whether they are content with current policies or if they would recommend a change. If students will not be able to receive full credit for work that occurred during an unexcused absence or suspension, ensure this is clear in policies. Also indicate the amount of times that teachers will be required to allow students to turn in makeup work for excused absences, unexcused absences, and suspensions.

If your school, district, or state mandates reductions in course credits or grades in secondary school due to truancy, ensure that your policies clearly explain how these reductions work. Provide frequent education for students and families and increase monitoring of truancy so that students and families can be forewarned about the consequences of continued absenteeism and the school can implement interventions before a student fails courses. Students should never reach the point of having to retake courses, repeat a grade, or enroll in summer school because they were unaware that absenteeism would lead to course failure.

Indicate Measures the School Will Take When It Identifies Problematic Patterns of Attendance

Provide descriptions of procedures in place to assist students and families who are having difficulty maintaining regular attendance. For example, list supports that the school can offer when there are barriers to attendance or if the student experiences situations that make school aversive. Provide contact information for personnel who are available to support and problem-solve, such as school counselors, the student's teacher, administrators, and district support personnel.

Describe the school's procedures for intervening at Tiers 2 and 3 (see Chapters 10 and 11) and indicate measures the school may take to help the student and family address absenteeism. Clearly define the truancy court procedures or other punitive procedures that may be used as a last resort if the student and family do not demonstrate efforts to improve the student's attendance. In the wording and implementation of these procedures, be careful to balance two concerns: on one side, adhering to attendance policies and using punitive procedures when positive and proactive procedures alone are ineffective, and on the other side, remaining aware of the overwhelming barriers and challenges that many families face. Consider individual circumstances and situations when implementing procedures such as truancy court, and ensure that student and family efforts to improve are weighted significantly in decision making about how to proceed.

Continually Review and Revise Policies

Because student populations change and causes of absenteeism may also change across time, recognize that you may need to periodically revise your policies to ensure they are working for your students and parents. We recommend doing an annual policy review in conjunction with your attendance data, especially data from student surveys that help you understand common causes of absenteeism. If a common cause is clearly identified, it may be beneficial to do some initial universal prevention work, as described in previous chapters, by sharing information with students and parents, using motivational systems, or tailoring universal strategies. Then, if these strategies work, consider as a team whether policy revisions would help bolster and make the changes permanent, or if the strategy change is sufficient for the time being. It may also be necessary and beneficial to seek input from the whole staff or district personnel. If the strategies you implemented were not successful in improving attendance, consider whether a policy revision would increase the efficacy of the strategies because policies may be taken more seriously than strategies, or whether you need to try different strategies before considering a policy change.

The most important thing to recognize about your policies is that although they should be designed to reflect your school's attendance goals and procedures, they take time to revise. If your policies currently reflect a traditional punitive approach, focus primarily on truancy, or otherwise do not reflect your current school mission and beliefs about attendance, do not delay implementing strategies to build a culture of attendance while you wait for a policy change. Work over time to analyze and revise policies as you continue to do everything possible to prevent absences.

▪ ▪ ▪ ▪ ▪

This chapter wraps up the focus on universal prevention. The concepts we have discussed can solidify your attendance initiative by clarifying the initiative and related procedures through your written policies. As you proceed through the final two chapters on Tier 2 and Tier 3 intervention, recognize that the focus on universal intervention in this book was entirely purposeful. Although schools typically want to jump straight into intervening with students who are flagged as at-risk, we have found—and research supports—that most students will respond appropriately when schools provide an increased focus on universal procedures. The hope is that these efforts will significantly minimize the numbers of students in your school in the Severe Chronic Absence, Chronic Absence, or At-Risk Attendance categories. By using relatively easy, simple, and inexpensive universal strategies to tackle the problem, you create room for designing and delivering Tier 2 and Tier 3 interventions to students with concerns that are more resistant and complex.

■ ■ ■ ■ ■

Summary of Tasks Related to Analyzing and Revising Attendance Policies

Use the following summary as a quick reminder of the tasks involved in analyzing and revising your school's attendance policies.

Analyze existing policies.

- Identify existing policies for areas of strength and possible areas for revision.
- Work with the team, relevant school and district personnel, and other stakeholders (e.g., students, parents, community organizations), as appropriate, to develop recommendations for policy revisions.

Revise policies to reflect attendance goals and school procedures, following school and district guidelines for policy revision.

- Create a plan for how attendance policies will be taught and reviewed with staff, students, and families.
- Update any relevant documents (e.g., student handbook, website, staff handbook) to reflect policy changes.

Designing and Implementing Effective Early-Stage Intervention Approaches

Once your school has implemented effective universal prevention procedures at Tier 1, you can begin to identify students with more resistant attendance problems. Some of these students may have shown no improvement with universal procedures such as lessons and motivational systems. Others may have responded initially—their attendance improved for a short time and then began to decline again. These students require something more to sustain regular attendance patterns.

Relatively simple interventions should be tried first before moving to interventions that require more time and resources, such as those described in Chapter 11. When we ask schools what intervention looks like for students with resistant absenteeism problems, the response we often get is "home visits." A home visit is time and resource intensive, however, and simply a preliminary step in developing a comprehensive intervention plan. By themselves, home visits do little to address absenteeism issues. Furthermore, many schools have absenteeism problems that are so pervasive that it is not realistic or sustainable to attempt home visits for every student with attendance issues. Schools must work to reduce the number of students with attendance problems by using early-stage interventions and Tier 2 procedures.

The early-stage classroom interventions described in this chapter are delivered primarily by a classroom teacher, but school leaders need to know about, understand, and support the interventions. We also provide broad descriptions of a few Tier 2 interventions that offer targeted supports in a small-group setting or through predesigned options that an individual student can join at any time.

Train Teachers to Implement Early-Stage Classroom Interventions

Because teachers are the primary staff who interact with students, we recommend that they take the lead in the earliest stages of addressing an attendance problem with students and families. Teachers may feel uncomfortable implementing these procedures without support; therefore, plan to allocate professional development time or provide resources for staff on how to implement early-stage interventions such as phone calls home and planned discussion.

Have Teachers Make Initial Phone Calls Home

Whenever a student has been absent several days in a row or is identified as having a problematic pattern across a month or two, have teachers contact families with a phone call to discuss the problem. These calls should be welcoming and supportive. Emphasize that the student is missed when absent and that it is important for the student to be in class every day. Consider providing a guided script for teachers that allows them to preplan what they will say (see Figure 10.1 for an example).

If the student's attendance improves, encourage the teacher to follow up with parents and provide positive feedback and appreciation to the family for helping the student get to school each day. If the teacher makes one or more phone calls and determines that these calls are not making a difference, or the problems indicated by the family are beyond the teacher's knowledge or capacity to support, the teacher can request additional assistance from a school counselor, psychologist, behavior specialist, or problem-solving team. The teacher should remain involved in subsequent conversations and interventions as much as possible.

Implement Planned Discussions with Students

Note: The planned discussion described here is adapted from Intervention A in Interventions, *by Randy Sprick and Mickey Garrison (2008) and used with permission.*

FIGURE 10.1 **Guided Script for Early-Stage Phone Call Home**

Hello Mr./Ms. _____,

This is [insert student's name]'s teacher. How are you today?

I'm calling because I've noticed that [insert student's name] has been absent ____ times in the last month, and I want to make sure that everything is OK and that we are doing everything we can to support [insert student's name] being in school.

We really miss [insert student's name] when [he/she] is gone, and I especially miss [discuss student strengths].

At [insert school name], we are really working to make sure that every student in our school has the best opportunity for success, and we know that this happens when students are in school every day when they are not seriously ill. Our goal is that every student have fewer than nine absences across the school year because we know this gives them the best likelihood of success in school and beyond. However, we also know that it can be really difficult for students to be in school every day. We are committed to making sure that we work with each student and each family if there are any things that make it difficult for a child to be in school regularly.

Can you tell me why [insert student's name] has been absent and if there is anything that makes it particularly difficult for [insert student's name] to be in school?

- **If parents are reluctant to discuss the problem,** conclude by indicating that you are pleased when the student is in class and hope that the parents will reach out if there is anything you or the school can do to ensure that the student is present each day. Provide contact information for the school counselor and administrator.

- **If parents mention challenges that you can help problem solve,** spend time discussing ideas with them or schedule a follow-up call or conference at a convenient time. For example, if their child frequently complains about being sick but they don't know whether staying at home is warranted, guide them in how to use the "How Sick Is Too Sick for School" form (see Figure 7.7 on page 128). If the form indicates that the student should probably come to school, assure the parents that they should bring their child to school and let you know about the complaint. You will carefully monitor the child throughout the day and send the child home if the illness worsens.

- **If parents mention challenges that are beyond your capacity to support,** work to facilitate communication with the school counselor, administrator, or other personnel. Let parents know that you will remain a part of the problem-solving process as much as possible.

A planned discussion is a focused meeting with a student at a time that is free from distractions and interruptions. For students who have not responded to general classroom and schoolwide information about the importance of regular attendance, a private meeting with their teacher may convey the seriousness of the problem and show them that the teacher notices and cares when they are absent. Train teachers to prepare for their meeting using the following steps:

- **Determine when to meet individually with the student.** This meeting could occur during a well-managed independent work period when other students are highly engaged in an independent activity, or during lunch or recess. Be careful to schedule the meeting during a time when it will not feel punitive or the student will be distracted or rushing to get to the next activity. If needed, ask if an interventionist (perhaps the school counselor) can monitor your class for 10 minutes so you can have a private discussion with the student.

- **Plan to keep a written record of the discussion** (see Figure 10.2 for an example). Before the meeting, print a record of the student's attendance and make note of any specific points that you would like to discuss.

During the meeting, teachers should state their concerns, brainstorm actions that the student or staff can do to support the student and resolve attendance problems, and set up an informal action plan. Use these recommendations to guide the discussion:

- **Work to sensitively communicate concerns about attendance and get clarity from the student.** As you discuss the student's attendance record and your concerns, make it clear that you are not attaching blame or accusing the student, but rather looking for ways to collectively work together to problem solve. Encourage the student to share his or her perspective about challenges the student is facing in coming to school regularly. If the student is reluctant to discuss the situation or disclose reasons for absences, work together to look at the attendance record and identify patterns. For example, you might look at the reasons on the record for absences and gently probe for more information (e.g., "I see that you were excused for illness three times in October. Do you remember what was going on then?").

FIGURE 10.2 **Planned Discussion Record**

_____   _____   _____
Student   Teacher   Date

Describe the problem: Number of absences _____ Absence category _____

Provide specific description of reasons for absences and anything else discussed as part of the problem:

Brainstorm (*What can you do? What can I do? What can others do?*):

Select actions, and identify who will be responsible for doing each action:

Set up next meeting date and time:

_____

- **Brainstorm actions that you and the student can take to resolve attendance concerns.** Work with the student to create a list of ways that the student, teachers, the student's parents, the school, or community might help the student be in school regularly. Encourage the student to come up with as many ideas as possible—nothing is silly or out of the range of possibility when brainstorming. Let the student know that you will both come back to the ideas on the list when you work together to make a plan.

  A relevant example of this step involves a student we worked with who was having problems with peers on the bus, a situation that was causing him to avoid school. We worked with him to brainstorm a list of possible actions we could all take to solve the problem. Some of the possibilities included assigning a seat for him or the other students, identifying a bus buddy (an older peer to sit with), and looking for a carpool or walking school bus. These possibilities ranged from relatively simple solutions, such as the assigned seat, to things like the walking school bus that would require at least two adult volunteers and far more coordination and effort.

- **Set up an informal action plan.** Work with the student to pick a few actions on the brainstormed list that are manageable and likely to help. When possible, keep the plan relatively simple at this stage of intervention, and identify strategies that do not require a huge amount of involvement or change from other people, such as the student's parents or interventionists in the school. Strategies that help the student focus on the goal of regular attendance and demonstrate commitment and support by the teacher are especially beneficial. If additional efforts and personnel are warranted, work with the student to identify simple preliminary strategies that you can both start right away. Schedule a subsequent meeting with the student and other people identified as part of the plan.

  For the student in the school bus example, we discovered that he had a phone with music on it that he carried each day, but he had no headphones. He thought that if he could just listen to music and tune out the other students, the problem might go away. We let him borrow a pair of headphones to keep in his backpack, and we recommended that he sit near the bus driver, as the other students liked to sit at the back of the bus. Using these simple strategies helped reduce his anxiety about being on the bus, and he found that when he ignored the other students, they began to ignore him as well. He finished the remainder of the year on the bus without problems, and his attendance improved.

- **Schedule a follow-up meeting.** Schedule a follow-up meeting within two weeks of the initial discussion. Knowing that there will be a sustained effort to resolve the problem brings an increased sense of accountability and likelihood of action for you and the student. It also ensures that the student will be recognized for improvements and that the plan will be revised if needed. If the student continues to struggle with attendance, consider implementing other ideas that were brainstormed, and bring in additional problem-solving processes, personnel, and interventions as appropriate (see Tier 2 interventions in this chapter and Tier 3 approaches in Chapter 11).

Identify Students Who Require Tier 2 Support

To identify students who require Tier 2 supports, review red-flag procedures as described on pages 52–53 in Chapter 3. Even if a student has Severe Chronic Absence (missing 20 percent or more of school days), do not assume the student requires intensive intervention if you have not tried simple interventions. Perhaps small amounts of additional support will be enough to help change the attendance pattern.

Note that the attendance team may be in charge of identifying students who are not responding to universal procedures, but this team typically does not guide the intervention process for students in Tiers 2 and 3. Once students are identified, they should be referred to a student-support team or other multidisciplinary intervention support team that will determine appropriate interventions for the student and monitor the data and progress across time.

Design Tier 2 Support Systems

Within a multitiered system of support (MTSS) model, Tier 2 procedures are targeted interventions for students who have not responded to school-wide Tier 1 procedures, but they are not as time or resource intensive as Tier 3 procedures. Tier 3 supports should be reserved for students with the most resistant absenteeism problems (see Chapter 11 for a description of Tier 3 support systems).

Characteristics of Tier 2 Interventions

There is no universally accepted definition of Tier 2 procedures, but they typically include interventions that can be implemented quickly (within three to five days) once a need is identified. This means that procedures must be largely defined before identifying a specific student's attendance problem and that personnel are already trained and have needed materials. Some features of effective Tier 2 interventions include explicit instruction of skills, opportunities for students to practice skills in the natural setting, and frequent positive and corrective feedback (Anderson & Borgmeier, 2010). Examples of Tier 2 interventions include daily progress report interventions, such as check in/check out (CICO) procedures or Connections (both described later in this chapter), social skills groups (see the next paragraph for examples), small groups for academic instruction, and mentoring. Students can be plugged in to these existing interventions as soon as their needs are identified. Be cautious about placing groups of adolescent students with problematic behavior into small-group interventions, however, when no role models are present. Research indicates that interventions for high-risk youth that provide training in settings isolated from other peers (e.g., pull-outs) may actually increase problem behavior due to *deviancy training*— a situation in which the students in the small group reinforce one another for negative behavior (Dishion, McCord, & Poulin, 1999). When placing students who are older than 10 into small-group interventions, ensure that an equal or greater number of peer role models also participate.

The Tough Kid Social Skills Book (Sheridan, 2010) provides outlines for training sessions and recommended procedures for providing social skills training to students in grades 3 through 7. It addresses skill areas such as social entry and maintaining interactions, with specific skills such as how to join a conversation or recognize and express feelings when interacting with others. For students who have not learned how to get along successfully with others in social situations, school can be a highly aversive place, involving constant negative interactions with peers and adults. A student may actively avoid school or may miss school due to suspensions for inappropriate interactions with peers and adults. Procedures described in *The Tough Kid Social Skills Book* can be used with a small group, a whole class, or even the whole school. When designing a small group, consider the issue of deviancy training mentioned earlier and include positive peer role models. As noted by the author, "a group comprised of all really Tough Kids may not be a good idea . . . balance the group with some students whose problems are less severe" (p. 44). She recommends a group size of four to eight students who are within a two- to three-year age range and developmental level.

Although preliminary hypotheses about the cause of a student's absenteeism may be considered when deciding which interventions are appropriate, the initiation of a Tier 2 plan does not require a functional behavior assessment or other time-intensive planning and program design. Furthermore, although a problem-solving or student-support team may be involved in identifying interventions appropriate for students who need Tier 2 support, each intervention is typically run by one or two staff members rather than a multidisciplinary team.

Examples of Tier 2 Interventions

Small-group attendance advisory. Keithley Middle School in Washington State designed an attendance advisory class to support students whose absenteeism remained problematic despite schoolwide prevention efforts. For 22 minutes a day, four days a week, groups of 18 to 20 students identified with attendance problems met in their advisory class with one of the school counselors. During this time, students tracked their daily attendance and monitored their attendance rate (see Figure 10.3). The counselor checked in with students to look at their attendance records and provide positive feedback or problem-solving support as needed. When a student was absent from the group, the counselor or one of the students in the group phoned to tell the student he or she was missed and that everyone hoped to see the student soon.

Every month, the counselors designed a scope and sequence of lessons that focused on topics such as the importance of attendance, organizational

FIGURE 10.3 **Attendance Monitoring Form for Advisory Period**

Name: _____

My total number of absences last school year (20___/ 20 ___) were ___.

Current school year: 20 __ / 20 __. My goal is no more than ___ absences this school year.

Directions: Fill in the weekday calendar template with the dates that correspond with the current month. Pick a color for each attendance category and color in the days of the month using your coding.

Attendance category:

☐ I was at school all day ☐ I was tardy ☐ I left early ☐ I was absent all day

Month: _____ Year _____

Monday	Tuesday	Wednesday	Thursday	Friday	Record absences each week

Absences this month: _____   Total absences to date: _____

strategies for home and school, and ways to meet school and classroom expectations to increase success. They worked with students to identify and address challenges, such as what to do when they don't have needed school supplies and feel embarrassed. In this case, counselors helped students to identify ways to access available resources without feeling stigmatized, which led to increased efforts within the school to provide easy access to school materials. In the advisory meetings, students also focused on community building and working for group and individual incentives based on attendance.

Figure 10.4 illustrates the attendance for each student in the advisory class in the year before the intervention and after becoming part of the advisory. Notice that all but one student demonstrated a significant reduction in the number of absences during the school year, and almost all students were successful in moving into the Regular Attendance category.

Mentoring interventions. Mentoring interventions connect each student with a supportive and caring staff member (or other adult). They can be designed to address underlying causes of absenteeism by problem-solving transportation issues, helping the student complete school or homework or providing academic tutoring, or simply increasing the student's connectedness to school through a positive relationship with an adult.

FIGURE 10.4 **Attendance Advisory Results for Individual Students**

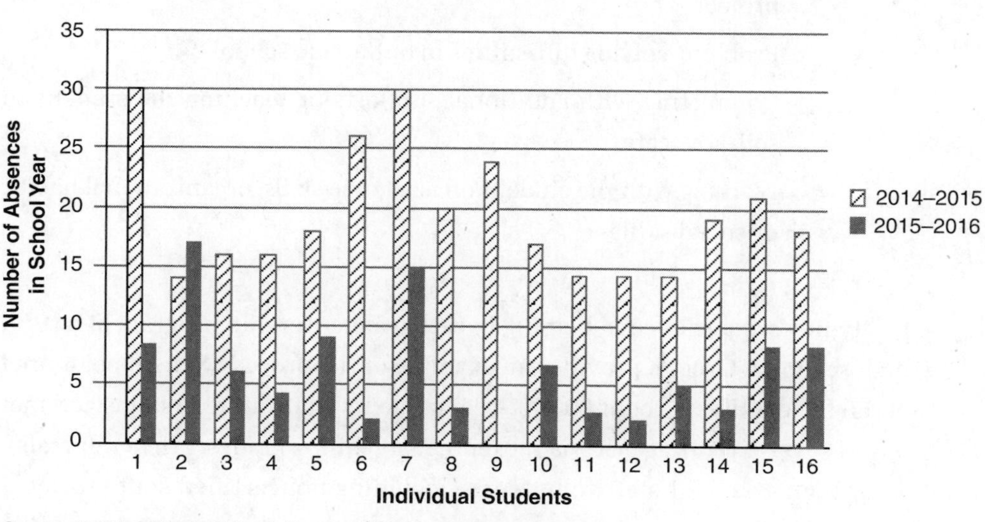

Source: Keithley Middle School, Tacoma, WA. Used with permission.

When designing a mentoring program, it is important to do the following:

- **Ensure that mentors have good interpersonal skills and are able to build a strong relationship with the student.** They should be able to meet consistently for regularly scheduled sessions at least once a week and commit to meeting for at least a year.

- **Ensure that one highly trained staff member (e.g., counselor, behavior interventionist, school psychologist) supervises and coordinates the intervention,** providing oversight for all mentor and mentee relationships through monthly check-ins and monitoring of data. Encourage mentors to keep an informal log of what occurs at each mentoring session that can be reviewed when they meet with the intervention coordinator.

- **Provide training for mentors on skills needed,** and work to identify activities that mentors may do during mentoring meetings, such as the following:
  - Identifying and celebrating student strengths and accomplishments
  - Working with the student to set academic or behavioral goals (e.g., behavioral contracting)
  - Providing positive incentives for growth through structured reinforcement systems
  - Working with the student on a school or community-based service project
  - Problem-solving difficulties in or outside school
  - Connecting with additional supports or teaching the student to self-advocate
  - Working with the student on academic skills, organizational habits, or social skills

Randy's experience in helping to set up a mentorship program at a rural high school in Oregon provides an example of the process. School personnel began by identifying about 30 first-year students who, in the first quarter, met any of several red-flag criteria (absenteeism, failing grades, office referrals). They then asked for staff volunteers—including noncertified staff—to serve as mentors. Mentorship would involve contacting the student and explaining mentorship as a way to have a staff member in the student's corner to help navigate the high school journey via brief weekly meetings. Twenty-six staff volunteered and were individually matched with students (the only criterion was that the student could not be in the mentor's class). About a month after the plan was initiated, Randy met with the mentors to get some feedback and provide some information on goal setting as one possible activity. One of the teachers said she did not think mentoring was working. When asked why, she said, "Well, I meet with her on Thursdays briefly after school, and all she does is sulk and respond to greetings, comments, or questions in monosyllables." Randy asked if the student came to her room on Thursdays, and she replied yes. He asked, "Does the student have to come?" She replied no. The fact that the student showed up even when it was not required clearly suggested to Randy that the student was finding some value in the program.

Four years after the mentoring program began, an article in the local paper profiled graduating students who attributed their success in high school to the support of a mentor. Although there are no formal data, anecdotally there were some great successes—including the student just described. All the students in the mentoring program whose families stayed in the community graduated on time.

Daily progress report. When struggles to succeed in school are due to behavioral issues or a lack of meaningful relationships with adults, a daily progress report can be used to increase the student's success and motivation to attend. These interventions may use a positive, supportive adult mentor (as described earlier) who greets the student at school each morning and gives the student a daily progress report form (see Figure 10.5). Throughout the day, the student receives brief feedback and a rating (e.g., 0, 1, or 2 points) from teachers and common-area supervisors on two or three specific behavioral goals (e.g., follow directions quickly, keep hands and feet to self, remain on task). At the end of the day or the following morning, the student reviews scores with the mentor and receives a reward if the daily point goal has been met. The mentor works with the student each day to celebrate successes or to problem-solve difficulties, and also graphs and reviews the student's progress over time.

In some schools, these kinds of interventions are called check in/check out, or CICO. *Connections* is a tool that uses a web-based system to eliminate

FIGURE 10.5 **Sample Daily Progress Report**

Name: Martin R.   **Date:** 2/8

Coordinator directions: Fill in the student's daily schedule and one to three specific behaviors for the student to work on. Also fill in the daily goal the student needs to meet in order to earn a reward.

Teacher directions: Rate the student on each behavior during your class using the rating scale in the box at the bottom left. Also indicate whether classwork and homework were complete and homework assigned. Note any homework that needs to be completed in the "Comments" section and initial the form where indicated.

Schedule	Behaviors to work on			Classwork Complete	Homework Complete	Homework Assigned	Comments	Teacher Initials
	Be on time	Turn in assigned homewk/classwk	Get attention in appropriate ways					
Science	0 1 ②	0 1 ②	0 1 ②	Ⓨ N	Ⓨ N	Y Ⓝ		
Math	⓪ 1 2	0 ① 2	0 ① 2	Ⓨ N	Y Ⓝ	Ⓨ N	Do word probs on p. 237	
Lang. Arts	0 1 ②	0 1 ②	0 1 ②	Ⓨ N	Ⓨ N	Ⓨ N	Read Ch 19, even questions	
Soc. Studies	0 1 ②	0 1 ②	0 1 ②	Ⓨ N	Ⓨ N	Ⓨ N	Study for test next Wed.	
	0 1 2	0 1 2	0 1 2	Y N	Y N	Y N		
	0 1 2	0 1 2	0 1 2	Y N	Y N	Y N		
	0 1 2	0 1 2	0 1 2	Y N	Y N	Y N		
	0 1 2	0 1 2	0 1 2	Y N	Y N	Y N		
	0 1 2	0 1 2	0 1 2	Y N	Y N	Y N		
Behavior totals	6	7	7	Total for all behaviors: 20				

I have reviewed the Daily Progress Report and discussed it with my child.

Parent signature: _____

Bonus for parent signature: _____   Daily goal: 19   Goal met? Ⓨ N

Rating Scale

0 = Student did not meet the expectation.

1 = Student met the expectation most of the time or responded quickly and appropriately to corrections.

2 = Student met the expectation all of the time with few or no reminders.

Source: From Absenteeism and Truancy: Interventions and Universal Procedures, by W. R. Jenson, R. Sprick, J. Sprick, H. Majszak, and L.Phosaly, 2013, Eugene, OR: Pacific Northwest Publishing. Copyright © 2013 by Pacific Northwest Publishing. Reprinted with permission.

the need for hand entry of student data in daily progress reports (see pacificnwpublish.com for details).

Meaningful Work. Meaningful Work is a school jobs program that helps meet students' basic needs for attention, belonging, and a sense of purpose. When students feel disconnected from school or have interests outside school that directly conflict with the requirements of school, they may need an increased sense of purpose to motivate them to attend. The program involves (1) identifying a range of jobs that require students to be at school each day, such as office mail sorter, fish feeder, playground equipment manager, visitor tour guide, flag raiser, coffee deliverer (for teachers), and (2) working to match each student with a job that is of high interest and helps meet the student's needs for recognition or social acceptance.

Some of the critical components for a Meaningful Work program include the following:

- Identifying a supervisor for each job who can work to develop a nurturing relationship with the student and can provide supportive, positive feedback and consistent contact
- Carefully matching the student with an appropriate job based on the student's age and need for direct supervision
- Providing training and needed materials for the supervisor
- Ensuring that the student receives sufficient training in all skills needed to be successful in the job

We heard one example of a school that had a partnership with a technology company that agreed to build a computer-repair area at the front entrance of the school. The idea was to train students to do simple technology fixes and computer maintenance, and staff members, students, or family members could come an hour before school to get technology assistance. Most students had to apply for these jobs, but some who needed additional positive attention and higher visibility in the school were directly recruited. They gained attention and skills during training, consistent positive interaction from the supervising staff member in the repair area, and lots of praise from those they helped. Although this example is a fairly sophisticated version of a Meaningful Work intervention, it clearly demonstrates how a school can get creative in thinking about ways to meet students' needs for attention, belonging, and a sense of purpose.

■ ■ ■ ■ ■

In this chapter we have described early-stage classroom interventions and Tier 2 interventions that can be implemented for students who have not responded to universal prevention efforts at Tier 1. For most students, we recommend trying these relatively simple interventions before proceeding to the time- and resource-intensive interventions described in Chapter 11, even if the student has a significant number of absences. For some students, an intervention like Meaningful Work or even a planned discussion may be sufficient to meet the student's needs and help emphasize the importance of attendance. If attendance continues to be problematic or gets better and then worsens again, the student likely has multiple complex factors or highly difficult factors contributing to absenteeism, and a more systematic, data-driven, and individualized approach is necessary. We describe such intensive intervention plans in the next chapter.

■ ■ ■ ■ ■

Summary of Tasks Related to Designing and Implementing Effective Early-Stage Intervention Approaches

The following summary can serve as a quick reminder of the tasks involved in designing and implementing effective early-stage intervention approaches.

Train teachers to implement early-stage classroom interventions.

- Identify early-stage interventions that classroom teachers will use (e.g., calls home, planned discussion).
- Determine who will provide information/training for teachers on how to conduct early-stage interventions, and identify when this will occur.

Design Tier 2 support systems.

- Determine how students who require Tier 2 intervention will be identified and flagged for support (see Chapter 3 for red flags).
- Identify who will be responsible for Tier 2 intervention planning (e.g., multidisciplinary team, student support team, problem-solving team).
- Create a range of Tier 2 interventions (e.g., attendance advisory, mentoring, daily progress report, Meaningful Work). Ensure that selected interventions are preplanned and ready to use so that a student can receive the Tier 2 support within three to five days.

11

Designing and Implementing Function-Based Approaches for Students with Ongoing Attendance Concerns

For students who do not respond to universal prevention and early-stage or Tier 2 interventions, continued absenteeism is a symptom of problems that are more resistant to change. These can differ vastly from student to student. One student may have a chronic illness, another may lack adequate supports at home, and another may be seeking to avoid frustration with academic deficits. For many students, multiple contributing factors work together to prevent regular attendance.

In this chapter we provide a broad overview of a function-based, or cause-based, approach. You can use this approach to determine the cause or causes of absenteeism for each student at Tier 3 and design individualized interventions to address each cause. For a more comprehensive resource for Tier 3 assessment and intervention, see *Functional Behavior Assessment of Absenteeism & Truancy* (Jenson et al., 2013). This kit includes functional behavior assessment (FBA) materials such as observation protocols, interviews, and records review forms that can help you identify causes of a student's chronic absenteeism and design an appropriate intervention plan. It also includes a copy of *Absenteeism & Truancy: Interventions and Universal Procedures* (Jenson et al., 2013), which includes step-by-step descriptions for 25 different interventions.

Identify Students Who Require Tier 3 Support

To identify students who require Tier 3 supports, review red-flag procedures as described on pages 52–53 in Chapter 3 and make note of students who have not responded to lower-level supports. Refer these students for Tier 3 problem solving. Because Tier 3 procedures require significant amounts of time and resources, reserve them for students who have the most persistent absenteeism problems. If you find that many students require Tier 3 support, reevaluate your universal and targeted systems to determine if you need to expand your efforts in the earlier tiers.

Planning for Tier 3 assessment and intervention is typically done by a multidisciplinary team that includes interventionists such as the counselor, school psychologist, behavior specialist, or social worker, and may involve one or more administrative and teaching personnel. Once an intervention plan is designed, it may involve a combination of interventionists, classroom teachers, parents, and outside agents (e.g., mental or physical health providers, department of human services personnel, rehabilitation services staff).

 Janelle's Experience

Note: This scenario illustrates the functional behavior assessment and intervention process.

Janelle was a kind, quiet 4th grade student. Although teachers occasionally expressed concerns about how reserved she was in classes, she never had visible behavioral challenges and only periodically struggled with academic skills, so she was never flagged for intervention. When the school began tracking chronic absence, however, Janelle's name came up in the Chronic Absence category. A little research showed Janelle had multiple years of chronic absence since kindergarten, with all absences excused by her mother.

The school initiated a conference with Janelle and her mother to discuss their concerns. The counselor talked with them about the importance of regular attendance, and Janelle's mother agreed that she would try to make sure Janelle went to school. Because there were no obvious causes for Janelle's absenteeism other than her mother letting her stay home from school whenever she asked, the team hoped that increasing the mother's commitment to regular attendance would solve the problem. However, to strengthen their Tier 2 intervention, they also had Janelle and her mom sign a behavioral contract and used a simple reinforcement system, allowing

Janelle to earn points toward a gift certificate for her favorite store when she attended regularly. These certificates were obtained using funds through the school's Positive Behavioral Intervention and Supports fund.

Janelle's attendance improved for a few weeks, but then the counselor learned that it had rapidly deteriorated. Even worse, Janelle's mom was still dropping her daughter off at school each day, but Janelle was sneaking out and walking back home. The counselor realized they were dealing with a more complex problem, so he referred Janelle to the multidisciplinary team for Tier 3 intervention planning.

Use Functional Behavior Assessment to Identify Causes of Absenteeism

Functional behavior assessment (FBA) is an evidence-based process used to determine why a student engages in a particular behavior. In general, FBAs involve defining problem behavior(s), identifying environmental and interactional events that predict and maintain the behavior, and creating an individualized support plan that addresses the contextual factors, skills deficits, and other causes that were determined to predict and maintain the problem behavior (McIntosh, Brown, & Borgmeier, 2008).

The FBA Process

To identify the function of absenteeism, gather data from multiple sources to develop a clear picture of the student's absenteeism or truancy. These data sources may include the following:

- Records review (attendance and disciplinary)
- Teacher, parent, and student interviews
- Home visits
- Observations in settings of concern at school or outside of school
- Academic screening and testing measures

To identify patterns in a student's absenteeism (e.g., time of day, time of year, subject), probe the various data sources and analyze the resulting data to determine the following:

- **Antecedents.** Consider whether the data indicate that the student's absenteeism is triggered by certain people, places, times, or activities.

For example, the student may be more likely to be absent on days when certain friends are also absent or suspended from school.

- **Setting events.** Setting events are events that occur at a different time or place before the absence. They reduce the likelihood the student will make positive choices and increase the likelihood of absence. For example, if a student has a fight with her parents the night before school, she may feel overwhelmed by school stressors and be unable to cope with attending.

The following anecdote can help to clarify the difference between antecedents and setting events.

Dylan was a 7th grader who was frequently suspended due to physical fights with male peers. As we analyzed the patterns of these fights, we found that the immediate antecedents were back-and-forth teasing and physical horseplay. At some point, Dylan would switch from playfully participating to perceiving these interactions as hostile, and then he would fight. We knew that on some days, he could engage in the teasing and physical horseplay without escalation, but on other days, he seemed to have a switch that would flip much more quickly. As we dug deeper, we realized that the difference had to do with how things were going at home. When Dylan was getting along with his dad and had had good interactions during visits with his mom (who was incarcerated), he was better able to cope with playful social interactions with peers. However, when his mom refused a visit or he struggled in his relationship with his dad, Dylan's tolerance at school was significantly reduced. We realized we would need to design an intervention plan that addressed both the immediate antecedents (helping him learn how to better engage and maintain social interactions with peers) and the setting events (helping to support him and teaching him coping strategies for his significant life stressors).

Information gathered from multiple data sources can help you identify any specific factors that should be incorporated into the design of the intervention plan. Consider this information as you analyze the data to develop a hypothesis about the function, or cause, of absenteeism. Ask questions such as these: What is preventing the student from attending? Why does the student or parent feel it is necessary to miss school? What benefit is the student getting out of being absent—what is serving to reinforce the absenteeism?

Remember that for many students with resistant absenteeism, numerous functions work together to cause the problem. Common functions include the following:

- Lack of understanding about the importance of attendance
- Barriers to attendance
- Escape or avoidance
- Desire to obtain or access something outside school
- Lack of value placed on school

See Figure 11.1 for a summary of some of the possible causes of absenteeism within each function. Note that these functions are identical to the common causes of absenteeism described in Chapter 8. Review pages 144–150 for more detailed explanation of some of these causes. Add to each of these categories as you identify functions of absenteeism for students in your school and community.

Dropout Prevention: An FBA Success Story

One principal shared with us a story about two students who were on a typical route to dropping out. Their behavioral concerns, academic deficits, and patterns of increasing absenteeism all pointed to a troublesome trajectory. At the beginning of the students' senior year, the staff initiated a full FBA, using the procedures in *Functional Behavior Assessment of Absenteeism & Truancy* (Jenson et al., 2013). The principal indicated that it took staff almost two months to conduct the interviews, observations, and records reviews. Although some of the data simply confirmed information they already knew (e.g., academic or social skills deficits), they also discovered home factors that were causing the students difficulty in school. At the end of the assessment process, the team had a comprehensive picture of the factors that were contributing to the students' struggles in school and causing them to disengage (e.g., lack of parental and sibling support, homelessness, making unhealthy choices outside school, lacking a positive connection to adults and peers at school). The staff designed intensive intervention plans that were intended to support the students in overcoming barriers and addressing disconnection from school, including a daily check-in with the principal or a teacher, meetings once a week with a family member, check-ins over the weekend to make sure the students were safe and had a place to stay, computer-based lessons for part of the school day, and efforts to make

FIGURE 11.1   **Functions (Causes) of Absenteeism to Consider When Designing Intervention Plans**

Lack of Understanding About the Importance of Attendance

- Parents or students don't recognize the negative effects of absenteeism
- The school does not place value on or emphasize the importance of attendance

Barriers to Attendance

- Chronic illness
    - Asthma
    - Chronic pain
    - Diabetes
    - Specify other _____
- Minor illness or somatic complaints
- Obesity
- Dental problems
- Mental health conditions
    - Depression
    - Anxiety
    - Behavioral disorder
- Transportation problems
    - Unreliable parent transportation
    - Missing the bus
    - Too far or unsafe to walk or bike
    - Inability to be bused from multiple residences
- Financial issues
    - Food insecurity
    - Lack of access to clothing or clean clothes
    - Unstable housing or homelessness
    - Specify other _____
- Pregnancy/teen parenting
- Parents unable or unwilling to help student get ready for school
- Work

(continued)

FIGURE 11.1 **(continued)**

- Caring for relatives
    - Siblings
    - Elderly family members
    - Parents
- Specify other _____

Escape or Avoidance
- Deficits
    - Academic
    - Social
    - Coping
- People
    - Conflict with students
    - Bullying situations
    - Conflict with staff
- Situations
    - Punitive climate
    - Unsafe climate
    - Chaotic climate
    - Boredom
    - Embarrassment
- Specify other _____

Desire to Obtain Something or Access Something Outside School
- Attention
    - Peer
    - Adult
- Access to tangible items or activities
    - Technology
    - Food
    - Games

FIGURE 11.1 *(continued)*

---

  o Sleep

  o Drugs/alcohol

  o Sexual activity

  o Illegal activity

- Specify other _____

Lack of Value

- Student, family, or community does not place value on school
- Student, family, community, or school does not view school as "suitable" for specific students
- Specify other _____

---

the students cultural role models in the community (e.g., taking elders food, leading camping trips).

At the end of the year, both students graduated. Although the principal acknowledged that this kind of intensive process could not be done with more than a few students a year, he attributed much of the success in this case to the comprehensive picture the school was able to develop through the FBA and the corresponding interventions it put in place.

Design and Implement Behavior Intervention Plans

Based on the findings of the FBA, develop preliminary hypotheses about the functions of absenteeism for the student and rank them by what appears to be the primary cause. Initial interventions should target the most important function. For example, a student may miss school primarily because he struggles with social interactions with peers, but a secondary function may be the opportunity to play video games all day. The initial intervention plan should provide support to help the student with social skills and building friendships with peers. Concurrently, a reward of time for video games based on attendance could be negotiated with the parents, or the school could set up a video game console for the student to use during lunch as a reward for improved attendance.

✓ **Janelle's Experience** The team began the FBA process for Janelle by interviewing her teachers. The team was eager to interview Janelle's 2nd grade teacher because Janelle had nearly perfect attendance that year, in direct contrast to her other years of school. They wanted to find out if this teacher did something different to encourage Janelle's attendance. The teacher said she noticed that Janelle developed a few close friendships but was extremely anxious about interacting with other peers and appeared especially fearful about things like large-group projects and having to speak in front of the whole group. Throughout the year the teacher worked hard to create comfortable opportunities for Janelle to participate (e.g., placing her in small-group experiences with her close friends and having her share responses privately with the teacher instead of in front of the class). When the team members observed Janelle in her current class, they noticed her body language became extremely tense when the teacher pulled Popsicle sticks to randomly call on students, and she frequently asked to use the restroom or get a drink of water to avoid being called on. Although other factors such as mild academic deficits were identified as possible contributing factors, the team hypothesized that the primary function of Janelle's absenteeism was unaddressed anxiety about being called on to participate in class.

Create a written record summarizing all the data collected from the FBA and clarify roles, responsibilities, and steps for selected interventions. Include the following information:

- **Clear description of behaviors of concern.** An example of a clear description is "Lacey has been absent 14 days excused and 6 days unexcused out of 100 days this year [20 percent]."

- **Contributing factors such as setting events and antecedents.** Highlight those that should be incorporated into the intervention plan design (e.g., if a difficult home situation contributes to absenteeism, design an intervention that provides a supportive mentor in the morning or includes practice in coping skills as soon as the student arrives at school so that the student can transition effectively into the school environment despite home stressors).

- **Hypothesized functions.** List these in order of what seems to be most motivating or prevalent in causing the absenteeism.

- **One or more interventions that address hypothesized function(s) and contributing factor(s).** Include details such as these:
  - ○ An observable and quantifiable goal for the intervention (e.g., Lacey will average no more than one day of absence each month—excused or unexcused—for the remaining four months of school. She will attend school at least 95 percent of the time).
  - ○ A detailed description of the interventions.
  - ○ Responsibilities of staff, family, and/or community agencies for carrying out the intervention, such as who will track data, check in with the student, and provide skills training. Set dates for when each responsibility will be initiated and completed.
  - ○ A plan for follow-up and review of the intervention. Ensure that an initial review of progress takes place after two weeks of implementation and that subsequent follow-up occurs at least once a month to review progress and make intervention decisions.
  - ○ Any forms or additional information that will be used to intervene (e.g., behavior contract form, daily progress report form, etc.).

✓ **Janelle's Experience** The team identified the following two antecedents as being the most prominent in Janelle's avoidance of school: (1) anxiety about being called on to participate in class and (2) having to participate in group experiences with peers who were not her close friends. The consequence of her absenteeism was escaping from anxiety. Therefore, the team designed an intervention plan that provided short-term escape for Janelle in the form of alternate means of participation, along with long-term work on coping skills and techniques for managing anxiety. They trained Janelle's teachers not to call on her in class unless they first asked her something such as this: "Janelle, that is a great response for number four. Would it be OK if I call on you to share your answer?" Janelle knew that her teachers would never ask her to speak out in class unless she gave permission, which they hoped would reduce her immediate levels of anxiety and enable her to come to school. The team also asked teachers to temporarily ensure that Janelle was placed in group activities with one or more of her preferred peers, and they designed times for Janelle to work with the counselor on basic coping skills for managing anxiety, such as deep breathing, muscle relaxation, and positive self-talk. The team created a clear record of all the steps of the intervention and who was responsible for training and management of the different components, and they agreed to meet two weeks later to review the progress of the plan.

Provide a copy of the completed behavior intervention plan to each person who will be involved in implementation. Meet with parents and the student to get needed permissions and to go over details of the intervention plan. As the plan progresses, update it as needed to reflect any interventions that may have been added if the student is not making adequate progress or to indicate when and how existing interventions will be diminished as the student experiences success.

Remember that resistant problems may require multiple concurrent interventions. Start by designing a plan that addresses the factors that are most likely contributing to the problem, and continue by developing increasingly complex and intensive plans if the initial interventions do not yield positive results, behavioral change occurs too slowly, or attendance problems return over time after some initial positive results.

Janelle's Experience Janelle's attendance improved with the intervention plan, but she still felt anxious about having to speak in class and was reluctant to have her teachers begin randomly calling on her to participate. Because the team knew that she would have to learn to spontaneously participate if Janelle was going to be successful as she progressed through school and into the workplace, they decided to intensify the intervention plan. The school psychologist began meeting with Janelle weekly for cognitive behavior therapy. The team also had Janelle sign a revised behavior contract that provided reinforcement for any of her attempts to participate in class. For example, if Janelle raised her hand to provide an answer or responded "yes" when a teacher asked if she would share her answer, she would receive a tally toward a gift certificate. Over the next year and a half, Janelle had regular attendance, and she gradually overcame her fears about speaking in front of others. By the time she went to middle school, she was comfortable having teachers randomly call on her and had developed coping skills for dealing with other moments of anxiety that might arise.

■ ■ ■ ■ ■

This chapter provided information about how to assess and implement a function-based, or cause-based, approach to address students with the most severe absenteeism problems. This approach can be incredibly powerful because it works to address the root causes of absenteeism and provides necessary supports to help students overcome obstacles that lead to absenteeism. The time-consuming nature of Tier 3 procedures, and the corresponding personnel needed to collect data and design and implement the intervention plans, demands that the efforts be reserved for students who did not respond to less intensive procedures. Any time your intensive intervention systems are overwhelmed by the number of students involved, consider ways to intensify your universal procedures (see Chapters 2–9) and early-stage and targeted interventions (see Chapter 10) to reduce the number of students who are referred for Tier 3 services.

▪ ▪ ▪ ▪ ▪

Summary of Tasks for Designing and Implementing Function-Based (Tier 3) Approaches

Use the following summary as a quick reminder of the tasks involved in designing and implementing function-based approaches for supporting students who have ongoing attendance concerns.

Use functional behavior assessment (FBA) to identify causes of absenteeism.

- Determine how students who require Tier 3 intervention will be identified and flagged for support (see Chapter 3 for red flags).
- Identify who will be responsible for Tier 3 intervention planning (e.g., multidisciplinary team, student support team, problem-solving team).
- Identify who has the skills to conduct FBA procedures or who can be trained in FBA (e.g., school psychologist, school counselor), and select individuals in the school who can guide the FBA process.
- Use FBA procedures to identify specific factors that contribute to absenteeism for each individual student identified for Tier 3 support.

Design an individualized behavior intervention plan for each identified student.

- Select intervention(s) that have the greatest likelihood of success.
- Clarify all parts of the intervention plan in a written record that will be shared with all relevant stakeholders.
- Conduct ongoing progress monitoring and follow-up to review data and make decisions on a regular basis.
- Make adjustments and scale back the intervention plan as appropriate.

Conclusion

Educators have long lamented student absenteeism and the difficulties that frequent absences cause for teachers, classes, and the educational system at large. In the past, however, they did little to address attendance issues in a comprehensive and systematic way. Many educators believed there wasn't much they could do to address a problem that stemmed mainly from parents. Educators may have felt that changing parent behavior was out of their reach, or that parents who failed to bring their children to school regularly just didn't care about education. In other cases, absenteeism was viewed as a lesser concern in comparison with academic deficits and behavioral disruptions. Nothing was done to address absenteeism until an individual student's situation was so severe the school could no longer ignore it, and then the approaches were primarily punitive.

This book advocates a shift in both mindset and strategies to address absenteeism. First, increasing student attendance is a goal that is absolutely within reach for school systems. This shift in mindset is essential so that educators do not abdicate responsibility or believe that attendance is a problem they have no control over. In our work supporting schools as they build a culture of attendance, we have seen that attendance is a highly malleable concern that educators have great power to influence. Schools where chronic absenteeism is a significant problem have expressed surprise that relatively simple strategies make such a huge difference in improving attendance across the whole student body. In reality, most students, parents, and staff will do the right thing when they are educated about school attendance priorities and provided with useful tools that empower them to meet expectations. This means that all stakeholders must understand how critical it is for all students to attend school regularly. Furthermore, educators must provide meaningful tools and supports that help students and parents overcome the obstacles that prevent coming to school and that motivate students to attend every day that they possibly can.

We also advocate applying proven approaches for changing behavior to the issue of absenteeism so that schools are not attempting to reinvent the wheel. Purely punitive approaches are not effective in changing behavior or improving academics. Likewise, waiting for a severe problem to emerge and then attempting to intervene is rarely effective—and this approach typically wastes valuable resources because severe problems require intensive intervention.

The strategies we advocate focus on moving away from solely punitive and reactive approaches to absenteeism. Instead, we look to apply multitiered approaches that are being used to improve behavioral and academic systems of support in schools across the United States. Within a multitiered support system, the primary focus is on providing a solid base of universal support at the schoolwide and classroom levels to ensure that the vast majority (80 to 90 percent) of students are able to meet expectations without requiring individual support. Universal strategies include educating students and families about the importance of attendance, using motivational systems to encourage attendance, and implementing tailored yet universal strategies to address common attendance concerns across a student body.

Continuing within the multitiered model, school staff may try early-stage interventions for students who fail to respond to Tier 1 supports. These interventions include planned discussions and preliminary supports to address barriers to attendance. If students continue to struggle, staff implement increasingly intensive interventions at Tier 2 and Tier 3, using data to monitor students' responses to intervention and to make meaningful decisions about next steps. Tiered intervention systems progress from those that are relatively simple and quick to those that are more data driven, more time and resource intensive, and designed to address specific functions, or causes, of absenteeism. Multitiered systems ensure that valuable staff resources are used wisely and that supports are put in place to identify and support each student at the appropriate level of need.

We strongly believe that attendance is a critical variable that schools must address. Although schools have many priorities to tackle, attendance is critical for student success, and if students are not in school, no other priority, initiative, or strategy can realize its full potential. Schools simply cannot ignore patterns of absenteeism. For students to be successful in school, they first have to *be* in school. For academic and behavioral initiatives to be successful, students have to be present enough to benefit from those efforts. We hope that the strategies and resources in this book have motivated you to tackle absenteeism and have given you the tools you need to build and support a schoolwide culture of attendance.

Appendix A:
Examples of Attendance
Improvement Plans

The following are examples of how two schools—an elementary school and a high school—implemented the approaches recommended in this book.

Barnes Elementary School Attendance Improvement Plan

Preplanning Phase

1. Begin working on attendance initiative within existing PBIS system (March through summer).

    A. Existing PBIS team begins work on universal and systems-level planning.

    B. Tasks

        i. Put excuses and biases aside and develop the following belief: Barnes can achieve a 95 percent attendance rate across the school year. Every student will attend at least 171 days of school, averaging no more than 1 missed day a month.

        ii. Teach the belief to staff: Present initial information on chronic absenteeism and Barnes data at a monthly staff meeting to define the problem and develop common vocabulary.

Teachers use part of the meeting to review average daily attendance for their own classes and sort their students into regular, at-risk, and chronic absence categories.

iii. Teach the belief to students: PBIS team members present the attendance belief to classrooms in class meetings and detail legitimate and illegitimate reasons for being absent. Attendance belief is tied to existing PBIS beliefs around Kindness, Safety, Responsibility, and Respect.

iv. PBIS team meet on work days (2 days during summer) to plan next year of implementation.

v. Initiative is introduced to staff during inservice day in August, prior to students starting.

Implementation Phase

1. Teach the attendance belief to all members of the school community.

   A. Teach families about attendance data and ramifications of missing school. Also, express the attendance belief and provide parents with strategies for improving their child's attendance through:

      i. Back-to-school night

      ii. PBIS parent night

      iii. Newsletters

      iv. Website

      v. Letters

      vi. Facebook

      vii. Reader board

      viii. Teacher contacts

   B. Inform the community that "Attendance matters!"

      i. Contact local paper to get article written on initiative.

      ii. Contact local sports clubs to talk about attendance with players.

      iii. Contact local churches to talk about attendance with congregation.

      iv. Contact physicians to discuss attendance with families.

      v. Contact local businesses to ask if they would hang posters in their business.

      vi. Present initiative to school board.

2. Provide recognition at multiple levels.

A. Individual student recognition:

i. ROAR earners: Regular Outstanding Attendance Recipients—students who miss no more than 1 day of school a month. Students are recognized at lunch by signing their grade-level ROAR book. Two students from each class are drawn from the ROAR book to have lunch on stage with the principal (partnering with McDonald's to provide Happy Meals).

ii. Students who miss no more than 9 days for the whole year attend ROARstock—end-of-year celebration with pizza, ice cream, and recess games against/with the teachers.

B. Classroom recognition:

i. Attend-a-Bear. Every class that meets their class goal earns a tally on their attendance sheet (goal initially set at 90 percent for each class, then increases across time). When they obtain 10 tallies, the class creates a piece to decorate their bear. Completed bears are displayed in the hallway, and the class earns a group reward.

C. Schoolwide recognition:

i. Bear Attendance path showcased in front of school. Each month, total number of days attended by all students are added to the Bear path, which leads to the Bear cave. The Bear needed 56,700 days of attendance to reach the cave in the first year.

ii. Attendance check-up visual. Large graph in front of the school depicting monthly ADA and whether the school reached the goal of 95 percent ADA for each month.

D. Family/Community recognition:

i. Big Bear BBQ. Invite all families and community members (mayor, police, fire department, church officials, physicians, etc.) to celebrate families whose students attended 95 percent of the time. All students and families may attend, but families of students with regular attendance will be recognized with certificates and prize drawings. Celebration will include BBQ food for all attendees and recess games.

3. Develop supports for struggling students (Tier 2 and Tier 3 procedures).

A. Create Attendance Team (principal, counselor, intervention specialist).

B. Team meets once a week for 30–60 minutes to problem-solve for students with attendance below 95 percent.

C. Students with attendance below 95 percent are discussed, and team decides on next steps. Support typically involves three phases:

    i. Classroom teacher calls family to make positive contact, indicating: "I'm worried about your child's attendance. What can I do to help him or her get to school?"

    ii. If the child continues to have attendance below 95 percent, an Attendance Team member contacts the family again to express concern and offer help.

    iii. If the child continues to fall below 95 percent attendance, a meeting is held with the classroom teacher, family, and at least one member of the Attendance Team. Appropriate interventions are selected and implemented.

D. Implement function-based approaches using *Functional Behavior Assessment of Absenteeism & Truancy* materials with small numbers of severely chronically absent students who have not responded to other supports at Tier 1 and Tier 2.

4. Monitor and share attendance data.

A. Run attendance reports every 2–4 weeks. Data is reviewed by PBIS team and Attendance Team.

    i. PBIS team monitors the "health" of the whole system and makes adjustments to universal teaching and recognition systems as needed.

    ii. Provide teachers monthly and yearly attendance data for each student in their class, including the ADA for the month as well as across the whole year.

    iii. Provide teachers a list of students across all grade levels who are struggling with attendance so that all staff can reinforce and praise those students when they attend school.

B. Present attendance data regularly at classroom meetings, Super BEAR Assemblies, the school website, Facebook, Back-to-School Night, Newsletter, Semester Attendance Letters, and PBIS Parent Night.

Source: Barnes Elementary School Attendance Improvement Plan. Adapted with permission Barnes Elementary School, Kelso, WA. Copyright © 2018 Barnes Elementary School.

Challenger High School Attendance Improvement Plan

"When we focus on improving attendance, students will focus on improving their attendance."

1. Create a "Challenger Attendance Team."

   A. Include two or three teachers, attendance secretary, social worker, and principal.

   B. Meet on the first Monday of each month.

   C. Tasks

      i. Provide follow-up survey of students in September:

         a. When you miss school, why don't you attend?

         b. Examine data for possible functions of student absenteeism.

            (1) Barriers

            (2) Lack of importance/understanding

            (3) Escape/avoidance

            (4) To obtain something

      ii. Review monthly attendance data:

         a. Average Daily Attendance for the year and month since last meeting: Pull data using district attendance management system reports.

      iii. Identify trends in the data.

      iv. Identify students of concern (10 percent + absenteeism, year and current month).

      v. Plan interventions:

         a. Tier 1: universal, schoolwide interventions and reward systems

         b. Tier 2 and 3 interventions for students of concern

      vi. Share attendance data and trends at monthly staff meetings.

      vii. Connect with local business partners for class and student incentives.

2. Publicize the Importance of Attendance with Students/Parents/ Families: Initial Kickoff

   A. Share goal of Regular Attendance (fewer than 9 days of absences in a school year) with parents and students:

      i. Intake meetings

      ii. Newsletters home

        iii. School website

        iv. Social media (Facebook and Twitter feeds)

    B. Parent letters:

        i. Kickoff letter and attendance tracking card (number of days missed and reasons)

        ii. "How sick is too sick?" checklist

3. Emphasize Goals and Acknowledge Improvements

    A. Classroom Attendance Graph

        i. Teachers graph Average Daily Attendance with first- and sixth-period classes on a daily basis

           a. Set an attendance goal (e.g., 12 students or more in class every day).

           b. Take data 5 minutes into first and sixth periods to emphasize the importance of being in school and class on time.

           c. Reward class when they have achieved the goal (12 students or more in class for 10 days).

        ii. Teachers develop Mystery Motivators to use with their classes to reward improvements in attendance:

           a. Brainstorm several no/low-cost motivators with students.

           b. Create prize cards (many no/low-cost, few high-cost items).

           c. Without students seeing, draw a prize card, place in envelope, and attach to attendance graph.

           d. When students meet 10 days at goal, open the Mystery Motivator envelope and reward class for meeting goal.

    B. School Attendance Graph

        i. Post and graph schoolwide Average Daily Attendance in the Student Lounge and Main Office on a daily basis.

        ii. X amount of improvement in Average Daily Attendance = root beer float party for the school.

4. Classroom/Staff Interventions

    A. Teachers welcome and greet students, especially on return from absence, on a daily basis. Teachers work to build strong relationships with students.

        i. We missed you! Our class isn't the same when you aren't here. Is everything OK?

        ii. Where were you yesterday?

B. All teachers will have an attendance graph and motivational system to use with 1st and 5th period classes.

C. Teachers help students take individual pride in how their personal attendance is contributing to their own goals and the class's goals.

D. All teachers will be expected to call families and/or the student when a student enters the "at-risk" category or has more than one absence in a week.

5. Student Recognition

A. Send a mailing to families of students who have made improvements or have good/great attendance each month.

B. Monthly attendance recognition:

   i. Regular Attendance (no more than 5 percent absences)

   ii. Improved Attendance (compared with previous month)

   iii. Perfect Attendance for the month

6. Interventions for Students with Chronic/Severe Chronic Attendance Problems

A. Referrals to Care Team (students with 10 percent + absenteeism)

B. Function-Based Assessments for students with 20 percent + absenteeism

   i. Social worker, counselor, and/or principal complete *Functional Behavior Assessment of Absenteeism & Truancy* procedures for each student.

   ii. Design and implement interventions using *Absenteeism & Truancy: Interventions and Universal Procedures* book.

   iii. Monitor student attendance.

   iv. Acknowledge and reward improvements.

Source: Challenger High School Attendance Improvement Plan. Adapted with permission from Challenger High School, Bethel, WA. Copyright © 2018 Challenger High School.

Appendix B: Ideas for Student Reinforcers

The following are ideas for schoolwide, classroom, and individual student incentives that can be selected for intermittent rewards or used within a structured reinforcement system. This list is not exhaustive, and staff can get creative when creating options for reinforcement. Work with your students to identify rewards that would be motivating for them.

Schoolwide

- Certificates of recognition (whole class, individual student) awarded at assembly
- Announcement of students of the day
- Publish names on a recognition board
- Special day (e.g., hat day, funky apparel day)
- Field or activity afternoon/day (e.g., carnival, wacky water day, spirit days)
- Special activity (e.g., dance, talent show, photo booth, DJ during lunch)
- Principal or other staff member who works with all students does a crazy activity (e.g., wear a crazy tie, pie in the face, buzz-cut hair, dress as a clown for a day)

- Invite a famous person to the school to speak
- Schoolwide BBQ event or provide a special food (e.g., root beer floats, sundaes)
- Coupons or vouchers for discounts or free items such as school store merchandise, school portraits, school yearbook, city bus, bowling alley or arcade, local restaurants, or coffee shops
- Discount or free admission to a local museum, zoo, festival, sports event, school function
- Movie night in the gym or auditorium

Classroom

- Class game (e.g., Heads-Up, Seven-Up, team competition with group video game, charades)
- Letter or postcards mailed home to congratulate class on achievement
- Extra recess or extended recess time
- Read aloud a book of students' choice
- Class party (e.g., confetti party, ice cream party, disco dance party)
- Quick goofy activity (e.g., make armpit noises for 30 seconds, have a snowball fight with recycled paper for 20 seconds)
- Free time (e.g., chat break at end of class, choice of activities for x minutes)
- Choose study buddies or where to sit for the day
- Field trip
- Class time in supervised computer lab, library, gym, or another classroom
- Permission to use cell phone, tablet, computer, or personal music device (with headphones) in class

Individual

- Recognition mailed home or positive phone call home (teacher or principal)
- Choice of seat for the day (e.g., teacher's chair or next to a friend)
- Have lunch with someone (e.g., lunch with the principal or teacher, lunch in special location in school with two friends)

- Art/school supplies or gift certificate to school store
- Small item (e.g., hand stamp, sticker, temporary tattoo, Silly Putty toy, pencils/erasers, bubbles, action figure, sports or game trading cards, sunglasses, hair ornaments, comic book, or Mad Libs party game)
- Be a helper for someone (principal, custodian, librarian, specialist)
- Decorate a ceiling tile, wall, or sidewalk
- Help prepare an activity (e.g., plan assembly, teach lesson, create YouTube video)
- Discount or free admission to activity (e.g., rock climbing wall, ice rink, aquarium, sporting event, movie)
- Record a message for school or teacher's answering machine or video for school website
- First choice of activity or first in line (e.g., lunch line, lab activity)
- Play a game or do preferred activity for x amount of time

References

Ad Council. (2015). *California school attendance research project.* Retrieved from www.attendanceworks.org/wordpress/wp-content/uploads/2017/01/Ad -Council-QualitativeResearchReport-062015.pdf

Alexander, K. L., Entwisle, D. R., & Horsey, C. S. (1997). From first grade forward: Early foundations of high school dropout. *Sociology of Education, 70*(2), 87–107.

American Psychological Association. (n.d.). *Bullying and school climate.* Retrieved from www.apa.org/about/gr/issues/cyf/bullying-school-climate.aspx

Anderson, C., & Borgmeier, C. (2010). Tier II interventions within the framework of school-wide positive behavior support: Essential features for design, implementation, and maintenance. *Behavior Analysis in Practice, 3*(1), 33–45.

Applied Survey Research. (2011). *Attendance in early elementary grades.* San Francisco: Attendance Works.

Attendance Works and Everyone Graduates Center. (2017). *Portraits of change: Aligning school and community resources to reduce chronic absence.* Retrieved from www.communitiesinschools.org/media/filer_public/95/f6/95f642aa -6c65-4ed2-aa46-15b8977625e3/attendance-works-portraits-of-change -main-document-final-sept-1.pdf

Balfanz, R., & Byrnes, V. (2012). *Chronic absenteeism: Summarizing what we know from nationally available data.* Baltimore, MD: Johns Hopkins University Center for Social Organization of Schools.

Balfanz, R., Fox, J. H., Bridgeland, J. M., & Bruce, M. (2013). *Grad nation community guidebook, Tool 9, Attendance Survey.* Retrieved from http://guidebook .americaspromise.org/wp-content/uploads/2015/08/Tool-9-Attendance.pdf

Balfanz, R., Herzog, L., & Mac Iver, D. J. (2007). Preventing student disengagement and keeping students on the graduation path in urban middle-grades schools: Early identification and effective interventions. *Educational Psychologist, 42*(4), 223–235.

Baltimore Education Research Consortium (BERC). (2011). *Destination graduation: Sixth grade early warning indicators for Baltimore City Schools: Their prevalence and impact.* Baltimore, MD: Author.

Barge, J. (2011). *Student attendance and student achievement*. Atlanta, GA: Georgia Department of Education.

Black, A. T., Seder, R. C., & Kekahio, W. (2014). *Review of research on student non-enrollment and chronic absenteeism: A report for the Pacific Region* (REL 2015–054). Washington, DC: U.S. Department of Education, Institute of Education Sciences, National Center for Education Evaluation and Regional Assistance, Regional Educational Laboratory Pacific. Retrieved from https://ies.ed.gov/ncee/edlabs/regions/pacific/pdf/REL_2014054.pdf

Blazer, C. (2011). *Chronic absenteeism in the elementary grades* [Information Capsule 1009]. Miami, FL: Miami–Dade County Public Schools Research Services.

Brundage, A. H., Castillo, J. M., & Batsche, G. M. (2017). *Reasons for chronic absenteeism among secondary students*. Retrieved from www.floridarti.usf.edu/resources/format/pdf/NationalAggregateRCAReportFinal.pdf

Buehler, M. H., Tapogna, J., & Chang, H. N. (2012). *Why being in school matters: Chronic absenteeism in Oregon public schools*. Retrieved from www.attendanceworks.org/wordpress/wp-content/uploads/2012/02/Oregon-Research-Brief.pdf

Byrnes, V., & Reyna, R. (2012). *Summary of state level analysis of early warning indicators*. Baltimore, MD: Everyone Graduates Center.

Carr, E. G., Dunlap, G., Horner, R. H., Koegel, R. L., Turnbull, A. P., Sailor, W., . . . Fox, L. (2002). Positive behavior support: Evolution of an applied science. *Journal of Positive Behavior Interventions, 4*(1), 4–16.

Centers for Disease Control and Prevention. (2014, June). *Most recent asthma data*. Retrieved from www.cdc.gov/asthma/most_recent_data.htm

Chang, H. N., & Jordan, P. W. (2011). Tackling chronic absence starting in the early grades: What cities can do to ensure that every child has a fighting chance to succeed. *National Civic Review, 100*(4), 6–12. doi: 10.1002/ncr.20078

Chang, H. N., & Romero, M. (2008). *Present, engaged, and accounted for: The critical importance of addressing chronic absence in the early grades*. Retrieved from National Center for Children in Poverty website: www.nccp.org/publications/pdf/text_837.pdf

Connolly, F., & Olson, L. S. (2012). *Early elementary performance and attendance in Baltimore City Schools' pre-kindergarten and kindergarten*. Baltimore, MD: Baltimore Education Research Consortium.

Dalun, Z., Willson, V., Katsiyannis, A., Barrett, D., Song, J., & Jiun-Yu, W. (2010). Truancy offenders in the juvenile justice system: A multicohort study. *Behavioral Disorders, 35*(3), 229–242.

Dishion, T., McCord, J., & Poulin, F. (1999). When interventions harm: Peer groups and problem behavior. *American Psychologist, 54*, 755–764.

Dryfoos, J. G. (1990). *Adolescents at risk: Prevalence and prevention*. New York: Oxford University Press.

Easton, J. Q., & Engelhard, G., Jr. (1982). A longitudinal record of elementary school absence and its relationship to reading achievement. *Journal of Educational Research, 75*(5), 269–274.

Ehrlich, S. B., Gwynne, J. S., Pareja, A. S., & Allensworth, E. M. (2013). *Preschool attendance in Chicago Public Schools: Relationships with learning outcomes and reasons for absences.* Chicago: University of Chicago Consortium on Chicago School Research.

Farrington, D. P. (1996). Later life outcomes of truants in the Cambridge Study. In I. Berg & J. Nursten (Eds.), *Unwillingly to school* (4th ed., pp. 96–118). London: Gaskell/Royal College of Psychiatrists.

Finck, J. B. (2015). *When students miss school: The high cost to Houston.* Houston, TX: Barbara Bush Houston Literacy Foundation. Retrieved from s3.amazonaws.com /bushhoustonliteracy-webassets/When-Students-Miss-School-Final-1.pdf

Finn, J. D. (1989). Withdrawing from school. *Review of Educational Research, 59*(2), 117–142.

Fredericks, J. A., Blumenfeld, P. C., & Paris, A. H. (2004). School engagement: Potential of the concept, state of the evidence. *Review of Education Research, 74*(1), 59–109. doi: 10.3102/00346543074001059

Garry, E. M. (1996). *Truancy: First step to a lifetime of problems.* Washington, DC: Office of Juvenile Justice and Delinquency Prevention, U.S. Department of Justice.

Get Schooled Foundation. (2012). *Skipping to nowhere: Students share their views about missing school.* Retrieved from Attendance Works website, www.attendanceworks.org/wordpress/wp-content/uploads/2013/10 /Skipping-to-Nowhere-August-2012.pdf

Ginsberg, A., Chang, H., & Jordan, P. (2014). *Absences add up: How school attendance influences student success.* Retrieved from Attendance Works website, www.attendanceworks.org/absences-add-up/

Gottfried, M. A. (2009). Excused versus unexcused: How student absences in elementary school affect academic achievement. *Educational Evaluation and Policy Analysis, 31*(4), 392–415.

Gottfried, M. A. (2010). Evaluating the relationship between student attendance and achievement in urban elementary and middle schools: An instrumental variables approach. *American Educational Research Journal, 47*(2), 434–465.

Gottfried M. A. (2014). Chronic absenteeism and its effects on students' academic and socioemotional outcomes. *Journal of Education for Students Placed at Risk, 19*(2), 53–75.

Gottfried, M. A. (2015). Chronic absenteeism in the classroom context: Effects on achievement. *Urban Education*, 1–32. doi: 10.1177/0042085915618709

Griffin, B. W. (2002). Academic disidentification, race, and high school dropouts. *The High School Journal, 85*(4), 71–81.

Hallfors, D., Vevea, J. L., Iritani, B., Cho, H., Khatapoush, S., & Saxe, L. (2002). Truancy, grade point average, and sexual activity: A meta-analysis of risk indicators for youth substance use. *Journal of Social Health 72*(5), 205–211.

Hammond, C., Linton, D., Smink, J., & Drew, S. (2007). *Dropout risk factors and exemplary programs.* Clemson, SC: National Dropout Prevention Center, Communities in Schools.

Harvard Health Publishing. (2015, January). *Relaxation techniques: Breath control helps quell errant stress response.* Retrieved from www.health.harvard.edu /mind-and-mood/relaxation-techniques-breath-control-helps-quell -errant-stress-response

Henry, K. L., & Huizinga, D. H. (2007). Truancy's effect on the onset of drug use among urban adolescents placed at risk. *Journal of Adolescent Health, 40*(4), 358.e9–358.e17 doi: 10.1016/j.jadohealth.2006.11.138

Hernandez, D. J. (2011). *Double jeopardy: How third-grade reading skills and poverty influence high school graduation.* New York: Annie E. Casey Foundation.

Hibbett, A., Fogelman, K., & Manor, O. (1990). Occupational outcomes of truancy. *British Journal of Educational Psychology, 60*(1), 23–36.

Jenson, W. R., Rhode, G., Evans, C., & Morgan, D. (2013a). *The tough kid principal's briefcase.* Eugene, OR: Pacific Northwest Publishing.

Jenson, W., Sprick, J., Sprick, R., Majszak, H., Phosaly, L., Evans, C., . . . & Teplick, C. (2013). *Functional behavior assessment of absenteeism and truancy.* Eugene, OR: Pacific Northwest Publishing.

Jenson, W., Sprick, R., Sprick, J., Majszak, H., & Phosaly, L. (2013). *Absenteeism and truancy: Interventions and universal procedures.* Eugene, OR: Pacific Northwest Publishing.

Kane, J. (2006). School exclusions and masculine, working-class identities. *Gender and Education, 18*(6), 673–685.

Kearney, C. A. (2008). School absenteeism and school refusal behavior in youth: A contemporary review. *Clinical Psychology Review, 28*(3), 451–471.

Kerr, J., Price, M., Kotch, J., Willis, S., Fisher, M., & Silva, S. (2011). Does contact by a family nurse practitioner decrease early school absence? *Journal of School Nursing, 28*(1), 38–46. doi: 10.1177/1059840511422818

Kieffer, M. J., Marinell, W. H., & Stephenson, N. S. (2011). *The middle grades student transitions study: Navigating the middle grades and preparing students for high school graduation.* New York: Research Alliance for New York City Schools.

Levin, H. M., & Belfield, C. R. (2007). Educational interventions to raise high school graduation rates. In H. M. Levin & C. R. Belfield (Eds.), *The price we pay: Economic and social consequences of inadequate education* (pp. 177–199). Washington, DC: Brookings Institution Press.

Loeber, R., & Farrington, D. (2000). Young children who commit crime: Epidemiology, developmental origins, risk factors, early interventions, and policy implications. *Development and Psychopathology, 12*(4), 737–762.

Mac Iver, M. A. (2010). *Gradual disengagement: A portrait of the 2008–09 dropouts in the Baltimore City Schools* [Research report]. Baltimore, MD: Baltimore Education Research Consortium. Retrieved from http://baltimore-berc.org/pdfs/Gradual%20Disengagement%20final.pdf

Maynard, B. R., Salas-Wright, C. P., & Vaughn, M. G. (2015). High school dropouts in emerging adulthood: Substance use, mental health problems, and crime. *Community Mental Health Journal, 51*(3), 289–299.

Mayo Clinic. (2014, May 8). *Relaxation techniques. Try these steps to reduce stress.* Retrieved from www.mayoclinic.org/healthy-lifestyle/stress-management/in-depth/relaxation-technique/art-20045368

McIntosh, K., Brown, J. A., Borgmeier, C. J. (2008). Validity of functional behavior assessment within a response to intervention framework: Evidence, recommended practice, and future directions. *Assessment for Effective Intervention, 34*(1), 6–14.

Musser, M. P. (2011). *Taking attendance seriously: How school absences undermine student and school performance in New York City*. New York: Campaign for Fiscal Equity.

National Institutes of Health. (2010). Reading difficulty and disability [Fact sheet]. Retrieved from https://report.nih.gov/NIHfactsheets/Pdfs /ReadingDifficultyandDisability(NICHD).pdf

Nauer, K., White, A., & Yerneni, R. (2008). *Strengthening schools by strengthening families: Community strategies to reverse chronic absenteeism in the early grades and improve supports for children and families*. New York: Center for New York City Affairs, The New School.

Neild, R. C., Balfanz, R., & Herzog, L. (2007). An early warning system. *Educational Leadership, 65*(2), 28–33.

NIDCR (2018, February). *Dental caries (tooth decay) in adolescents (age 12 to 19)*. Retrieved from https://www/nidcr/nih/gov/research/data-statistics /dental-caries/adolescents

Pourat, N., & Nicholson, G. (2009). *Unaffordable dental care is linked to frequent school absences*. Los Angeles: UCLA Center for Health Policy Research.

Project Achieve. (2017). Project Achieve [website]. Retrieved from http:// projectachieve.info/

Reid, K. C. (1981). Alienation and persistent school absenteeism. *Research in Education, 26*(1), 31–40.

Reid, K. C. (1982). The self-concept and persistent school absenteeism. *British Journal of Educational Psychology, 52*(2), 179–187.

Reid, K. C. (1983). Institutional factors and persistent school absenteeism. *Educational Management and Administration, 11*, 17–27.

Robins, L. N., & Ratcliff, K. S. (1980). The long-term outcome of truancy. In L. A. Hersov & I. Berg (Eds.), *Out of school: Modern perspectives in truancy and school refusal* (pp. 65–83). New York: Wiley.

Rocque, M., Jennings, W. G., Piquero, A. R., Ozkan, T., & Farrington, D. P. (2016). The importance of school attendance: Findings from the Cambridge Study in Delinquent Development on the Life-Course Effects of Truancy. *Crime & Delinquency, 63*(5), 592–612. doi: 10.1177/0011128716660520

Romero, M., & Lee, Y.-S. (2007). *A national portrait of chronic absenteeism in the early grades*. New York: National Center for Children in Poverty.

Rouse, C. E. (2007). Quantifying the costs of inadequate education: Consequences for the labor market. In C. R. Belfield & H. M. Levin (Eds.), *The price we pay: Economic and social consequences of inadequate education* (pp. 99–124). Washington, DC: Brookings Institution Press.

Rumberger, R., & Thomas, S. (2000). The distribution of dropout and turnover rates among urban and suburban high schools. *Sociology of Education, 73*(1), 39–67.

Schwarz, R. (2016, June 15). 8 ground rules for great meetings. *Harvard Business Review*. Retrieved from https://hbr.org/2016/06/8-ground-rules-for-great-meetings

Sheldon, S. B., & Epstein, J. L. (2004). Getting students to school: Using family and community involvement to reduce chronic absenteeism. *School Community Journal, 14*(2), 39–56.

Sheridan, S. M. (2010). *The tough kid social skills book*. Eugene, OR: Pacific Northwest Publishing.

Smink, J., & Reimer, M. S. (2005). *Fifteen effective strategies for improving student attendance and truancy prevention*. Clemson, SC: National Dropout Prevention Center Network.

Sparks, S. D. (2010). Districts begin looking harder at absenteeism. *Education Week, 30*(6), 1, 12–13.

Sprick, R. (2017). *START on time!* (2nd ed.). Eugene, OR: Pacific Northwest Publishing.

Sprick, R., & Garrison, M. (2008). *Interventions*. Eugene, OR: Pacific Northwest Publishing.

Sprick, R., Garrison, M., & Howard, L. (2002). *Foundations: Establishing positive discipline policies* (2nd ed.). Eugene, OR: Pacific Northwest Publishing.

Sprick, R., Isaacs, S., Booher, M., Sprick, J., & Rich, P. (2014). *Foundations: A positive and proactive behavior support system* (3rd ed.; Modules A–F). Eugene, OR: Pacific Northwest Publishing.

Steiner, R. J., & Rasberry, C. N. (2015). Brief report: Associations between in-person and electronic bullying victimization and missing school because of safety concerns among U.S. high school students. *Journal of Adolescence, 43,* 1–4. https://doi.org/10.1016/j.adolescence.2015.05.005

Sugai, G., & Horner, R. (2006). A promising approach for expanding and sustaining school-wide positive behavior support. *School Psychology Review, 35*(2), 245–259.

U.S. Department of Education Office for Civil Rights. (2016). *Civil rights data collection (CRDC) for the 2013–14 school year.* Retrieved from https://www2.ed.gov /about/offices/list/ocr/docs/crdc-2013-14.html

Utah Education Policy Center, University of Utah. (2012). *Research brief: Chronic absenteeism.* Retrieved from www.schools.utah.gov/file /723cd525-40e2-4ab7-81a2-fb829d686b7b

Index

Note: The letter *f* following a page number denotes a figure.

About the Authors

 **Jessica Sprick** has a master's degree in special education and is a consultant and presenter for Safe & Civil Schools, as well as a writer for Ancora Publishing. Ms. Sprick has been a special education teacher for students with behavioral needs and dean of students at the middle school level. Her practical experience in schools drives her passion to help school and district staff develop and implement effective behavioral, academic, and attendance approaches. Ms. Sprick is the lead trainer for Safe & Civil Schools' model of absenteeism prevention and intervention, and she is a coauthor of the following attendance resources: *Functional Behavior Assessment of Absenteeism & Truancy* and *Absenteeism & Truancy: Interventions and Universal Procedures*.

Ms. Sprick is also a coauthor of *Foundations: A Proactive and Positive Behavior Support System* (3rd ed.), *Functional Behavior Assessment of Bullying*, and *Bullying: Universal Procedures and Interventions*. She may be reached at www.safeandcivilschools.com/aboutus/contact_us.php.

Dr. Randy Sprick has worked as a paraprofessional, a teacher, and a teacher trainer at the elementary and secondary levels. Author of widely read books on behavior and classroom management, Dr. Sprick is director of Safe & Civil Schools, a consulting company that provides professional development throughout the United States for teachers, administrators, and other school personnel. He and colleagues at Safe & Civil Schools work with numerous large and small school districts on longitudinal projects to improve student behavior and motivation. Dr. Sprick was the recipient of the 2007 Council for Exceptional Children (CEC) Wallin Lifetime Achievement Award.

His publications include *Leadership in Behavior Support, CHAMPS: A Proactive and Positive Approach to Classroom Management, Discipline in the Secondary Classroom, Foundations: A Proactive and Positive Behavior Support System, Teacher's Encyclopedia of Behavior Management, START on Time!,* and *Coaching Classroom Management.* Dr. Sprick may be reached at www .safeandcivilschools.com/aboutus/contact_us.php.

Related ASCD Resources: Leadership

At the time of publication, the following resources were available (ASCD stock numbers in parentheses).

Print Products

10 Steps to Managing Change in Schools: How do we take initiatives from goals to actions? (ASCD Arias) by Jeffrey Benson (#SF115072)

100+ Ways to Recognize and Reward Your School Staff by Emily E. Houck (#112051)

Accountability for Learning: How Teachers and School Leaders Can Take Charge by Douglas B. Reeves (#104004)

Analytic Processes for School Leaders by Cynthia T. Richetti and Benjamin B. Tregoe (#101017)

The Art of School Leadership by Thomas Hoerr (#105037)

Design Thinking for School Leaders: Five Roles and Mindsets That Ignite Positive Change by Alyssa Gallagher and Kami Thordarson (#118022)

Five Levers to Improve Learning: How to Prioritize for Powerful Results in Your School by Tony Frontier and James Rickabaugh (#114002)

Improving Student Learning One Principal at a Time by Jane E. Pollock and Sharon M. Ford (#109006)

Leading Change Together: Developing Educator Capacity Within Schools and Systems by Eleanor Drago-Severson and Jessica Blum-DeStefano (#117027)

Learning from Lincoln: Leadership Practices for School Success by Harvey Alvy and Pam Robbins (#110036)

School Culture Rewired: How to Define, Assess, and Transform It by Steve Gruenert and Todd Whitaker (#115004)

For up-to-date information about ASCD resources, go to www.ascd.org. You can search the complete archives of *Educational Leadership* at www.ascd.org/el.

ASCD myTeachSource®

Download resources from a professional learning platform with hundreds of research-based best practices and tools for your classroom at http://myteachsource.ascd.org/

For more information, send an e-mail to member@ascd.org; call 1-800-933-2723 or 703-578-9600; send a fax to 703-575-5400; or write to Information Services, ASCD, 1703 N. Beauregard St., Alexandria, VA 22311-1714 USA.

WHOLE CHILD
TENETS

1 **HEALTHY**
Each student enters school healthy and learns about and practices a healthy lifestyle.

2 **SAFE**
Each student learns in an environment that is physically and emotionally safe for students and adults.

3 **ENGAGED**
Each student is actively engaged in learning and is connected to the school and broader community.

4 **SUPPORTED**
Each student has access to personalized learning and is supported by qualified, caring adults.

5 **CHALLENGED**
Each student is challenged academically and prepared for success in college or further study and for employment and participation in a global environment.

The ASCD Whole Child approach is an effort to transition from a focus on narrowly defined academic achievement to one that promotes the long-term development and success of all children. Through this approach, ASCD supports educators, families, community members, and policymakers as they move from a vision about educating the whole child to sustainable, collaborative actions.

School Leader's Guide to Tackling Attendance Challenges relates to the **safe, engaged,** and **challenged** tenets. *For more about the ASCD Whole Child approach, visit* **www.ascd.org/wholechild.**